To

From

Date

The Capacity of A Man

THE CORNERSTONE PUBLISHING

Joseph Olowe

The Capacity of A Man

Paperback ISBN: 978-1-944652-63-0

eBook 978-1-944652-69-2

Published by:
Cornerstone Publishing
A Division of Cornerstone Creativity Group LLC
Info@thecornerstonepublishers.com
www.thecornerstonepublishers.com

516.547.4999

Author's Contact

For booking to speak at your next event or to order bulk copies of this book please use information below:

P. O Box 10499
El Paso, TX 79995
1-800-561-9170 or +1 915-478-8807
www.drjosepholowe.com | info@drjosepholowe.com

DEDICATION

This book is dedicated to a giant in the faith — Pastor E.A. Adeboye — a man endowed with an unusual grace for enlargement. 'Grandpa' (as my wife and I like to call you) only eternity will unveil the impact of the impartation you gave us in Chicago while you laid hand on us. May you finish strong, sir.

ACKNOWLEDGMENTS

I will like to appreciate my savior Jesus Christ from whom all blessings flow. My sincere gratitude to my wife and partner in ministry, Omolade for her relentless pursuit of excellence for our family first and ministry.

To my children Olamide, Simi and Dare who have given me an opportunity to practice what I am preaching.

To my ministry team, first to my able editor who I consider as a gift from heaven to me, Pastor Joseph Ola and to Daniel Emonido who I refer to as mighty Danny, for all the divine graphics; many thanks. To Pastor Gbenga Showunmi and his professional team at Cornerstone Publishing, thank you for making this dream come true.

To a good friend of mine, Pastor David Olayemi — the first man apart from my family, who sincerely believed in my writing gift and encouraged me to pursue my dream — may the God of heaven never forget your labor of love.

CONTENTS

Dedication....5

Acknowledgments....7

Introduction....11

1. The Carrier of God....15
2. The Representative of God....29
3. The Enforcer of God's Will....43
4. The Mouthpiece of God....55
5. The Commander of God's Army....67
6. The Epitome of God's Power....77
7. The Custodian of All God's Resources....89
8. The Closer of God's Plan....101
9. The Epitome of God's Creation....113
10. God's Original Creation....127
11. The Man With Answers....135
12. A Praising Machine....145

INTRODUCTION

"The Lord thy God in the midst of thee is mighty; he will save, he will rejoice over thee with joy; he will rest in his love, he will joy over thee with singing." (Zephaniah 3:17 KJV)

The above Scripture say, "*The Lord thy God in the midst of thee is mighty...*" — that's a powerful thought! It implies amongst other things that God has come down to fellowship with men. When God comes down He does mighty things. According to Zephaniah 3:17, when God comes down, He saves, rejoices over us with joy, allows us to rest in His love and will even bring down the host of heaven — the angelic orchestral — to rejoice over us with singing. God will throw you a party!

If you are looking for what heaven on earth looks like, turn to this verse. The idea of God coming to fellowship with us makes it all worth to be on His side, but that is not the full gist. King Solomon shared another dimension with regards to God coming down — not only to fellowship but also to stay with us — to dwell with man on earth permanently.

> *"But will God in very deed dwell with men on the earth? behold, heaven and the heaven of heavens cannot contain thee; how much less this house which I have built!" 2 Chronicles 6:18 KJV*

King Solomon was so enthused about the idea of God dwelling with man, that he asked a serious question during the dedication of the temple he built in Jerusalem. "WILL GOD IN VERY DEED DWELL WITH MEN ON EARTH"? Great question! Here is a man who had experienced divine visitations, but each time God visits him, it was always a short stay — God coming in the cool of the day or visiting men with particular information. But on this occasion, King Solomon caught a glimpse of something that has never been revealed to man at the time — the idea of God staying permanently on earth dwelling WITH men. The God Who the heaven and the heaven of heavens cannot contain — massive, immeasurable, unquestionable, unquantifiable and endless — has decided to come down to dwell with men in a house of brick and mortar. As a result of that presence, after the trumpeters and singers ministered in unison, the house was filled with a cloud — the cloud of glory. The priests were not able to stand to minister because of the presence of the shekinah glory of God.

All these foreshadowed and revealed God's plan which is to come through Jesus, the mediator of a better covenant. The idea of God dwelling with man is unfathomable and inconceivable, but through Jesus it became possible for

God — not just to dwell WITH men but also to dwell IN men. King Solomon talked about a physical house hosting God, but metaphorically, he was referring to us as revealed by Peter in the New Testament: we are lively stones built up into a spiritual house, an holy priesthood to offer up spiritual sacrifices (praise and worship) which is acceptable to God by Jesus... What a divine transition from dwelling with us to dwelling in us. My question then is this: "what is the true capacity of a man carrying an unquantifiable God'?" UNQUANTIFIABLE!

> *"To whom coming, as unto a living stone, disallowed indeed of men, but chosen of God, and precious, Ye also, as lively stones, are built up a spiritual house, an holy priesthood, to offer up spiritual sacrifices, acceptable to God by Jesus Christ." 1 Peter 2:4-5 KJV*

> *"It came even to pass, as the trumpeters and singers were as one, to make one sound to be heard in praising and thanking the Lord; and when they lifted up their voice with the trumpets and cymbals and instruments of musick, and praised the Lord, saying, For he is good; for his mercy endureth for ever: that then the house was filled with a cloud, even the house of the Lord; So that the priests could not stand to minister by reason of the cloud: for the glory of the Lord had filled the house of God." 2 Chronicles 5:13-14 KJV*

More answers to come.

Happy reading.

CHAPTER ONE

THE CARRIER OF GOD

The divine intentions of God at the beginning was for us to be like Him — little gods. Everything He created was very good and on the sixth day He created MAN in His own image and after His likeness, male and female. As a goat gives birth to a goat and an elephant produces after its kind, every living creature produces after its image and likeness.

Something terrible happened however in the garden that sowed the seed of corruption into the human race, but the same event paved way for God to dwell in us, and we eventually become THE CARRIERS OF GOD! All these can be traced back to what happened when the serpent — the most subtle of the creatures — visited with Eve in the garden of Eden. That serpent — also called the devil — has not ceased roaming and roaring, seeking whom he might continue to deceive. His main trick is still to twist the Word of God to suit his purpose. That was his trick on Eve.

He asked Eve a very tricky question… *"Yea, has God said, ye shall not eat of every tree of the garden?" "That is not true at all, God gave all the herbs and the beasts as food to us"*, Eve answered cleverly. Then the devil went for the kill. Eve told the devil what God had said, *"but of the tree in the midst of the garden, we shall neither touch nor eat, lest we die."* The serpent answered the woman, *"ye shall not surely die…"* From their conversation, it became clear that if anyone negotiates God's Word with the devil, the devil will always win, because it shows that such a person is in doubt.

The devil then introduced an explanation — *"God knows that in the day you eat thereof, then your eyes shall be opened, and ye shall be as gods, knowing good and evil"*. Lie! Had God not already created them (and us) like gods? They didn't need to become what they already were — and neither do we. Every time the devil gets us to believe his lie, we lose big! On that very day, the devil robbed the entire humanity of our godlike nature. In our first parents, we traded our standing with God for a piece of fruit. In this chapter however, my goal is to present to us that through the sacrifice of Jesus on the cross, we have finally regained our godlike nature and has become a house in which God dwells in.

> *"And God said, Let the earth bring forth grass, the herb yielding seed, and the fruit tree yielding fruit after his kind, whose seed is in itself, upon the earth: and it was so. And the earth brought forth grass, and herb yielding seed after his kind, and the tree yielding fruit, whose seed was in itself, after his kind: and God saw that it was good. And God created great whales, and every living creature that moveth, which the waters brought forth abundantly, after their kind, and every winged*

fowl after his kind: and God saw that it was good. And God said, Let the earth bring forth the living creature after his kind, cattle, and creeping thing, and beast of the earth after his kind: and it was so. And God said, Let us make man in our image, after our likeness: and let them have dominion over the fish of the sea, and over the fowl of the air, and over the cattle, and over all the earth, and over every creeping thing that creepeth upon the earth. So God created man in his own image, in the image of God created he him; male and female created he them." Genesis 1:11-12, 21, 24, 26-27 KJV

"Now the serpent was more subtil than any beast of the field which the Lord God had made. And he said unto the woman, Yea, hath God said, Ye shall not eat of every tree of the garden? And the woman said unto the serpent, We may eat of the fruit of the trees of the garden: But of the fruit of the tree which is in the midst of the garden, God hath said, Ye shall not eat of it, neither shall ye touch it, lest ye die. And the serpent said unto the woman, Ye shall not surely die: For God doth know that in the day ye eat thereof, then your eyes shall be opened, and ye shall be as gods, knowing good and evil." Genesis 3:1-5 KJV

WHAT SPIRIT IS IN A MAN?

"But there is a spirit in man: and the inspiration of the Almighty giveth them understanding." Job 32:8 KJV

"But there is a spirit in man..." What a revelation God gave to a young man called Elihu. What is that spirit in a man? The spirit in a man is simply God in a man — God is that Spirit, and the Bible tells us in John 4:24 that God is a Spirit and they that worship him must worship in spirit and truth. This revelation did not only reveal to us that God is the Spirit, but also that we the worshippers are essentially 'a spirit' as well, because for our worship to be acceptable it MUST come out of our spirit man. As such, God is being worshipped by gods — what an elevation in status for us! Jesus revealed to us in the new testament, "that which is born of the flesh is flesh and that that which is born of the Spirit is spirit." In other words, for every believer, we have been declared a spirit, and the inspiration of the Almighty gives us an understanding of our divine nature through the better covenant Jesus brought us by His blood.

> *"God is a Spirit: and they that worship him must worship him in spirit and in truth." John 4:24 KJV*

> *"Jesus answered, Verily, verily, I say unto thee, Except a man be born of water and of the Spirit, he cannot enter into the kingdom of God. That which is born of the flesh is flesh; and that which is born of the Spirit is spirit." John 3:5-6 KJV*

WHERE IS THE TREASURE?

God commanded the light to shine out of darkness, and that light now shines in our hearts. Our heart is the dwelling place of God who now lives inside of us. We know from God's Word that He is the true light which lights every man that comes into the world, and this is the light that gives us the real life. God has given us the light of the knowledge of the glory of God in the face of Jesus

Christ, which is Christ in us the hope of Glory. Here is the good news all of this heavenly treasure is packaged in earthen vessels. What a mystery that God has decided to dwell on earth permanently in us — jars of clay. God has always desired to live in us from the beginning. When we were formed He gave us the BREATH OF LIFE, which is the life that God lives on and that life of God brought life into us. God is the treasure in our earthen vessel, that the excellency of the power may be of God, and not of us. This revelation has kept me very humbled because it is not about me — it's not about any of us — but it is a rare privilege that God dwells in us!

> *"For God, who commanded the light to shine out of darkness, hath shined in our hearts, to give the light of the knowledge of the glory of God in the face of Jesus Christ. But we have this treasure in earthen vessels, that the excellency of the power may be of God, and not of us." 2 Corinthians 4:6-7 KJV*

> *"In him was life; and the life was the light of men. And the light shineth in darkness; and the darkness comprehended it not. That was the true Light, which lighteth every man that cometh into the world." John 1:4-5, 9 KJV*

WHO ARE YOU?

King David also caught the revelation of who we are in Jesus. When God promised him that a seed of his will forever sit on the throne of Israel, he was privileged to have the foreknowledge of the mystery of Christ in us being the hope of glory. David declared that God is in the 'congregation of the mighty'. That is a revelation into our identity — we are the mighty ones! We picked that up from one of the attributes of our Almighty God who judges 'among the gods'. By revelation, David declared that we are gods — children of the most High. But out of our ignorance not realizing our position and the implications of God dwelling in us on earth, every affliction that troubles the people of the world will attempt to challenge our sonship in God. As a result, many believers are dying like ordinary men and falling like one of the princes — just like the devil fell from his previous status in heaven. So who are you? You are gods — sons of the most High!

> *"God standeth in the congregation of the mighty; he judgeth among the gods. I have said, Ye are gods; and all of you are children of the most High. But ye shall die like men, and fall like one of the princes." Psalms 82:1, 6-7 KJV*

Jesus corroborated this revelation in John 10:34-36 declaring that we are gods unto whom the word of God came — even the Word which was God from the beginning.

> *"Jesus answered them, Is it not written in your law, I said, Ye are gods? If he called them gods, unto whom the word of God came, and the scripture cannot be broken; Say ye of him, whom the Father hath sanctified, and sent into the world, Thou blasphemest; because I said, I am the Son of God?" John 10:34-36 KJV*

WHERE IS THE KINGDOM OF GOD?

The kingdom of God is where God dwells. For generations past, man had always been curious regarding the location of God's throne. Even the Pharisees asked Jesus about this when they had the chance, and contrary to the kind of response they were anticipating, Jesus amazed all the listeners.

> *"And when he was demanded of the Pharisees, when the kingdom of God should come, he answered them and said, The kingdom of God cometh not with observation: Neither shall they say, Lo here! or, lo there! for, behold, the kingdom of God is within you." Luke 17:20-21 KJV*

While they were expecting Him to say something about the kingdom of God being in heaven or in some other far away place, He said the kingdom of God does not come by observation, neither shall anyone tell you that it is here or there, because the kingdom of God is within them — within you and I. If the kingdom of God is where God abides, then the kingdom of God is right inside of us. This is why God expects us to worship Him always, as the twenty four elders do praising and worshiping Him 24/7.

> *"The four and twenty elders fall down before him that sat on the throne, and worship him that liveth for ever and ever, and cast their crowns before the throne, saying, Thou art worthy, O Lord, to receive glory and honour and power: for thou hast created all things, and for thy pleasure they are and were created." Revelation 4:10-11 KJV*

TO THE UNKNOWN GOD

Paul the Apostle was speaking to the Athenians and strangers. He observed that they were highly devoted people and that one of their altars of worship had an inscription: 'TO THE UNKNOWN GOD' — an apt description for the God that many believers are, as a matter of fact, serving — a God that is very far away from them. The good news today is that God is dwelling in your inside. Paul said since the foundation of the earth after the fall of man, men have been seeking after God as though He's far from us. Yes, it was because our sin separated us from Him, but now because of His divine choice, by His election, He has brought us close so that now, in Him we live, and move, and have our being, because we are His offsprings through Jesus. What a mystery! If we live and move in Him, then He must be dwelling in us. He's no longer an unknown God but a God that has declared His identity to us. It does not yet appear what we shall be, but we shall be like Him when we see Him face to face.

> *"For as I passed by, and beheld your devotions, I found an altar with this inscription, TO THE UNKNOWN GOD. Whom therefore ye ignorantly worship, him declare I unto you. God that made the world and all things therein, seeing that he is Lord of heaven and earth, dwelleth not in temples made with hands; Neither is worshipped with men's hands, as though he needed anything, seeing he giveth to all life, and breath, and all things; And hath made of one blood all nations of men for to dwell on all the face of the earth, and hath determined the times before appointed, and the bounds*

of their habitation; That they should seek the Lord, if haply they might feel after him, and find him, though he be not far from every one of us: For in him we live, and move, and have our being; as certain also of your own poets have said, For we are also his offspring. Forasmuch then as we are the offspring of God, we ought not to think that the Godhead is like unto gold, or silver, or stone, graven by art and man's device. And the times of this ignorance God winked at; but now commandeth all men everywhere to repent:" Acts 17:23-30 KJV

"Beloved, now are we the sons of God, and it doth not yet appear what we shall be: but we know that, when he shall appear, we shall be like him; for we shall see him as he is." 1 John 3:2 KJV

HOW CAN I BECOME A CARRIER OF GOD?

1. Be Born Again.

Anyone that wants to come to God must first believe that He is, and that He is a rewarder of them that diligently seek him. And how do we come to Him? Jesus answered that age-long question when He said to Nicodemus, *"Verily, verily, I say unto you, except a man be born again, he cannot see the kingdom of God."* How can I become born again? God has made this process very simple, viz: Acknowledge your sin and ask God for forgiveness. You can say these words to yourself as you read on:

"Lord Jesus, come into my heart. Be the Lord of my life. I declare you as Lord and I have decided to forsake the world to follow you. Thank You Jesus for saving me."

It is that easy! You are now born of the spirit — a spirit being! You are now a God-carrier. Congratulations on this milestone, which is the beginning of an awesome journey with Christ.

> *"But without faith it is impossible to please him: for he that cometh to God must believe that he is, and that he is a rewarder of them that diligently seek him." Hebrews 11:6 KJV*

> *"Jesus answered and said unto him, Verily, verily, I say unto thee, Except a man be born again, he cannot see the kingdom of God. Nicodemus saith unto him, How can a man be born when he is old? can he enter the second time into his mother's womb, and be born? Jesus answered, Verily, verily, I say unto thee, Except a man be born of water and of the Spirit, he cannot enter into the kingdom of God. That which is born of the flesh is flesh; and that which is born of the Spirit is spirit. Marvel not that I said unto thee, Ye must be born again. The wind bloweth where it listeth, and thou hearest the sound thereof, but canst not tell whence it cometh, and whither it goeth: so is every one that is born of the Spirit." John 3:3-8 KJV*

2. Consume The Word Of God.

Now that you have taken the first step of confessing Jesus as your Lord and personal Saviour, you have now become a carrier of God. It is time to grow up in your knowledge of God so as to know your inheritance in this new family of Christ. John wrote that in the beginning was the word, and the word was with God and the word was God. For us to grow and take up more of God's nature, we must become students of the word and proceed from feeding on the milk of the word to enjoying the meat of it. It is only through the Word that we can grow. Prophet Jeremiah looked for the word of God and found them — and ate them (that is, he meditated, read and practiced the Word), and the Word brought joy and rejoicing. The spirit of God comes into us through the Word! It is only the Word that will set our feet on the solid ground which is Christ Jesus.

> *"In the beginning was the Word, and the Word was with God, and the Word was God. The same was in the beginning with God." John 1:1-2 KJV*

> *"Thy words were found, and I did eat them; and thy word was unto me the joy and rejoicing of mine heart: for I am called by thy name, O Lord God of hosts." Jeremiah 15:16 KJV*

> *"And the spirit entered into me when he spake unto me, and set me upon my feet, that I heard him that spake unto me." Ezekiel 2:2 KJV*

3. Through Prayers.

Prayer is very important in the life of any Christian. It is our only means of communicating with God. We are encouraged in scripture to pray with all kinds of prayers, because through prayer the nature of God can fully develop in us. Paul the Apostle believed that the effective method to get a young Christian established in the knowledge of the indwelling Christ is by travailing in prayers. In Galatians 4:19, Paul prayed for his converts in Galatia that Christ be formed in them and for the reality of God dwelling in believers to become evident in their Christian walk with the Lord. He travailed in prayer for these to happen.

A series of questions were asked in the book of Isaiah 66:8; Who has heard such a thing? Who has seen such things? Shall the earth be made to bring forth in one day? Or shall a nation be born at once? Then came the answer — for as soon as Zion travailed, she brought forth her children. The nature of God is borne through prayers! All things are possible to a praying man or woman! The attributes of God living on the inside are manifested in our closets at our place of prayers.

> *"Praying always with all prayer and supplication in the Spirit, and watching thereunto with all perseverance and supplication for all saints;" Ephesians 6:18 KJV*

> *"My little children, of whom I travail in birth again until Christ be formed in you," Galatians 4:19 KJV*

> *"Who hath heard such a thing? who hath seen such things? Shall the earth be made to bring forth in one day? or shall a nation be born at once? for as soon as Zion travailed, she brought forth her children." Isaiah 66:8 KJV*

4. Through Communion.

Jesus is the mediator of the better covenant. He had communion with His disciples at every opportunity He had to do it. Before His crucifixion He had communion. When He appeared to them after His resurrection, He had communion. Before He ascended to heaven, He had communion and commanded it to be done always in remembrance of Him. Why did Jesus do it quite often? Because it is one of the ways by which we can keep ourselves alive in God! He said *"this is my body given unto you..."* We are the product of what we eat, so if we eat the flesh and drink the blood of Jesus, then it goes without saying that we will eventually become like Jesus. Except we eat the flesh of the Son of man and drink His blood, we have no life in us. Whosoever eats His flesh, and drinks His blood have eternal life — the reality of God — in us and the assurance of this comes through communion. Jesus said "my flesh is meat indeed, and my blood is drink indeed. He that eats my flesh, and drinks my blood, dwells in me and l in him." Friends, that makes you a bonafide carrier of God, simply by taking communion often. To be more like Jesus, eat communion at every opportunity you have to eat it.

> *"And he took bread, and gave thanks, and brake it, and gave unto them, saying, This is my body which is given for you: this do in remembrance of me. Likewise also the cup after supper, saying, This cup is the new testament in my blood, which is shed for you." Luke 22:19-20 KJV*

> *"Then Jesus said unto them, Verily, verily, I say unto you, Except ye eat the flesh of the Son of man, and drink his blood, ye have no life in you. Whoso eateth my flesh, and drinketh my blood, hath eternal life; and I will raise him up at the last day. For my flesh is meat indeed, and my blood is drink indeed. He that eateth my flesh, and drinketh my blood, dwelleth in me, and I in him. As the living Father hath sent me, and I live by the Father: so he that eateth me, even he shall live by me. This is that bread which came down from heaven: not as your fathers did eat manna, and are dead: he that eateth of this bread shall live forever." John 6:53-58 KJV*

CHAPTER TWO

THE REPRESENTATIVE OF GOD

God created the heavens and the earth in six days and rested on the seventh having found an able representative to continue with the work of creation and be in charge of every created thing. God formed man out of the dust and breathed His nature — all His attributes — into man. God planted a garden in Eden and man became His representative. Everything that pertains to the garden is now subjected to man as God's representative beginning with the naming of all cattle, fowls of the air and every beast of the field — whatever Adam called them, that became their names.

However, as the story unfolds, man became corrupted through disobedience and God got disappointed about the situation in which man found himself. But the love of God for man is beyond measure. He still wanted to be with man on earth, but since it is impossible for Him to live in corruption, He put in place an alternative by encapsulating His presence in a box which was called the ARK OF COVENANT. The ark essentially became the representative of God's presence which allowed Him to dwell with man without living in corruption. God commanded Moses to build the ark according to the pattern revealed to him. God was very particular about the appearance and the wellbeing of His host. The content of the ark were symbolic of men's rebellion to God, but God still kept Himself in the ark under the tent.

Every time the ark comes into the company of the children of lsrael in battle, victory is guaranteed unless there was sin in their camp. Each time the enemy confiscated the ark, the ark defended itself — some it inflicted with hemorrhoids, and others (like Uzzah who touched the ark irreverently) it struck down. But that was a temporary arrangement. In the fullness of time, God selected one lady by the name of Mary. She was visited by an angel who told her that the Holy Spirit will overshadow her. l believe that the reason why the Holy Spirit had to overshadow her was for her cleaning and sanctification — for Jesus to dwell in that womb, it had to be purified from corruption, and to demonstrate that God will eventually get His way back into man.

Mary conceived and gave birth to Jesus who walked the earth with us; He was God with us in the flesh for thirty three and half years before His final plan to dwell in us was fulfilled, and our divine representation status was fully restored back to us without any controversy. And with that restoration comes the commitment of His power to us as believers. Hence, Jesus said "all the power in heaven and earth has been given to us."

"And the Lord God formed man of the dust of the ground, and breathed into his nostrils the breath of life; and man became a living soul. And the Lord God planted a garden eastward in Eden; and there he put the man whom he had formed. And out of the ground made the Lord God to grow every tree that is pleasant to the sight, and good for food; the tree of life also in the midst of the garden, and the tree of knowledge of good and evil. And the Lord God took the man, and put him into the garden of Eden to dress it and to keep it. And Adam gave names to all cattle, and to the fowl of the air, and to every beast of the field; but for Adam there was not found an help meet for him." Genesis 2:7-9, 15, 20 KJV

"And they shall make an ark of shittim wood: two cubits and a half shall be the length thereof, and a cubit and a half the breadth thereof, and a cubit and a half the height thereof." Exodus 25:10 KJV

"And when the ark of the covenant of the Lord came into the camp, all Israel shouted with a great shout, so that the earth rang again. And when the Philistines heard the noise of the shout, they said, What meaneth the noise of this great shout in the camp of the Hebrews? And they understood that the ark of the Lord was come into the camp." 1 Samuel 4:5-6 KJV

"And the angel answered and said unto her, The Holy Ghost shall come upon thee, and the power of the Highest shall overshadow thee: therefore also that holy thing which shall be born of thee shall be called the Son of God." Luke 1:35 KJV

MOSES BECAME A GOD UNTO PHARAOH

Moses was called by God to lead the children of Israel out of Egypt to the land of Canaan. He was a fugitive who earlier murdered an Egyptian and fled for his life. He was a common man who has lost his identity — a shepherd and a cattle rearer — until God called him out of a burning bush for the greatest assignment of his life. He was not aware of his status as 'a god' until God told him to be His representative. It's not that God couldn't come down to deal with Pharaoh Himself but it will be illegal for God to do so because He has set out all the course of the earth and named it man's domain. One of God's earliest revelations to Moses was to point him to his god-natured status; He said "I have made thee a god to Pharaoh." In other words, God was saying to Moses, "you can do with Pharaoh whatever pleases you." Moses brought ten plagues over the Egyptians until their armies were utterly destroyed in the Red Sea. This is Moses who, by the way, is not a partaker of the better covenant that we now enjoy — and not only are we partakers of the better covenant, but Jesus said of us that we are greater than John the Baptist.

> *"And the Lord said unto Moses, See, I have made thee a god to Pharaoh: and Aaron thy brother shall be thy prophet. Thou shalt speak all that I command thee: and Aaron thy brother shall speak unto Pharaoh, that he send the children of Israel out of his land." Exodus 7:1-2 KJV*

DANIEL, IN WHOM THE SPIRIT OF GOD LIVES

Daniel was a man of worth in the Babylonian kingdom. He became relevant in that pagan kingdom for over sixty five years without compromise. He and his friends had unimaginably demonstrated what it looks like for God to dwell with men on earth. He was conspired against regarding his relationship with God and he was thrown into the lion's den but he came out the next day without any scratch. The king declared that the God of Daniel should be worshipped in the entire kingdom. His three friends were thrown into the fiery furnace because they refused to bow to an image. The fire was heated seven times as usual, yet while they were in there, God showed up as the fourth man. How were they able to do all these? They were simply the representatives of God — gods to all the inhabitants of Babylon. They acknowledged this so much that the astrologers and magicians said concerning Daniel and his brothers that in them dwells the spirit of the holy gods. They were men of unique understanding and wisdom — the wisdom of the gods was found in them. They were able to interpret dreams, solve difficult problems and dissolve doubts. Those are divine qualities! Since they were representing God, every other demonic god bowed to them. Daniel became the head of the astrologers and magicians throughout the kingdom.

> *"There is a man in thy kingdom, in whom is the spirit of the holy gods; and in the days of thy father light and understanding and wisdom, like the wisdom of the gods, was found in him; whom the king Nebuchadnezzar thy father, the king, I say, thy father, made master of the*

magicians, astrologers, Chaldeans, and soothsayers; Forasmuch as an excellent spirit, and knowledge, and understanding, interpreting of dreams, and shewing of hard sentences, and dissolving of doubts, were found in the same Daniel, whom the king named Belteshazzar: now let Daniel be called, and he will shew the interpretation." Daniel 5:11-12 KJV

JOSEPH: A MAN DISCREET AND WISE

Joseph showed that there was something different about him from birth. He experienced unusual favor — like Jesus Who grew in wisdom and stature, and in favor with God and man. Joseph was an epitome of these virtues, it all began with a dream, and he told his dream to his father and brothers, when you know what others do not know, that puts you into a different category — that was Joseph's situation. It was Joseph's godlike nature that was manifesting all along but nobody understood it. As a result, he was sold to the Midianites, and later to Potiphar, an officer of Pharaoh. Through it all, *"the Lord was with Joseph..."* What a statement! God dwelled with Joseph; a god man! He was a prosperous man because everywhere he went to, God showed up. He was an able representative of God. He was lied against and later went to prison, but his story did not end till he later became the Prime Minister of the land. King Pharaoh described this God's representative as *"a man in whom the Spirit of God is..."* — in whom God dwells! With God in us and as His representatives, we become wonders unto men. Pharaoh said according to Joseph's word shall the land of Egypt be ruled — that's what God's representation is all about.

"And Jesus increased in wisdom and stature, and in favour with God and man." Luke 2:52 KJV

"And Joseph was brought down to Egypt; and Potiphar, an officer of Pharaoh, captain of the guard, an Egyptian, bought him of the hands of the Ishmaelites, which had brought him down thither. And the Lord was with Joseph, and he was a prosperous man; and he was in the house of his master the Egyptian." Genesis 39:1-2 KJV

"And Pharaoh said unto his servants, Can we find such a one as this is, a man in whom the Spirit of God is? And Pharaoh said unto Joseph, Forasmuch as God hath shewed thee all this, there is none so discreet and wise as thou art: Thou shalt be over my house, and according unto thy word shall all my people be ruled: only in the throne will I be greater than thou." Genesis 41:38-40 KJV

PETER, YOU ARE THE ROCK!

Peter was a fisherman — an ignorant and unlearned man, whose first encounter with Jesus was at the Sea. It has been a brutal day in the fishing world as the fish had refused to take the bait. Peter and his crew were about to shutdown the business for the day when Jesus showed up. He asked them to use their boat for a preaching engagement and afterward the unusual happened; Jesus asked Peter to launch into the deep for a catch. Peter hesitated for a moment but obeyed and the result was a boat sinking with the catch of the month! Jesus has saved the day and restored their hope. This event changed Peter's life forever. He became a disciple of Jesus from there on.

As one of Jesus' disciples, Peter appeared to be the right-hand-man of Jesus. On one fateful day, Jesus asked His disciples a question: "Whom say ye that l am?" That was the question that will change Peter's life forever! He answered and said "thou art the Christ, the Son of the living God." This revelation of who Jesus is ultimately changed Peter's status for eternity! Jesus said "flesh and blood has not revealed this to you, but my Father which is in heaven." Peter finally got the revelation of God dwelling among men. From that day forward, Peter became a representative of God on earth with certain authorities. Jesus said "You are Peter, and upon this rock (the revelation of Christ living with men) l will build my church and the gates of hell shall not be able to overcome it." Jesus told His disciples not to tell anyone about the revelation and He began to reveal to them the divine plans.

> *"And it came to pass, that, as the people pressed upon him to hear the word of God, he stood by the lake of Gennesaret, And saw two ships standing by the lake: but the fishermen were gone out of them, and were washing their nets. And he entered into one of the ships, which was Simon's, and prayed him that he would thrust out a little from the land. And he sat down, and taught the people out of the ship. Now when he had left speaking, he said unto Simon, Launch out into the deep, and let down your nets for a draught." Luke 5:1-4 KJV*

> *"He saith unto them, But whom say ye that I am? And Simon Peter answered and said, Thou art the Christ, the Son of the living God. And Jesus answered and said unto him, Blessed art thou, Simon Barjona: for flesh and blood hath not revealed it unto thee, but my Father which is in heaven. And I say also unto thee, That thou*

art Peter, and upon this rock I will build my church; and the gates of hell shall not prevail against it. And I will give unto thee the keys of the kingdom of heaven: and whatsoever thou shalt bind on earth shall be bound in heaven: and whatsoever thou shalt loose on earth shall be loosed in heaven." Matthew 16:15-19 KJV

HOW CAN I BECOME A BETTER REPRESENTATIVE OF GOD?

1. Be Sensitive.

"The Holy Spirit, whom the father will send in my name, He shall teach you all things, and bring all things to your remembrance." The job of the Holy Spirit is to make us sensitive to the move of God. Whenever we are not sensitive, it becomes very difficult to represent God well on earth. Sometimes, we deal with situations that require heaven's attention, and we are waiting on God for direction while God is actually asking us, *"What are you waiting for?"* That was the experience of Moses at the Red Sea. He was asking God what to do, and God was reminding him that he's got the 'rod of God' to do wonders with. He told Moses, "tell the people to go forward." When we are not sensitive enough to the move of God, Isaiah compared us to a deaf man who cannot hear or a blind man with eyes but cannot see. "Who is blind, but my servant? Or deaf as my messenger that l sent? Seeing many things, but we cannot observe and with open ears but not hearing." To better represent God, we must be quick to hear what is happening in the spiritual realm. Though Apostle Paul did a lot as an able representative of God to the gentile nations, he was sensitive enough to recognize when he was being forbidden by the Holy Ghost to preach the word in Asia. He yielded to the Spirit and went into Macedonia immediately, with a great harvest of souls waiting there. Doing the work of God, and being His representative on earth requires sensitivity.

> *"But the Comforter, which is the Holy Ghost, whom the Father will send in my name, he shall teach you all things, and bring all things to your remembrance, whatsoever I have said unto you." John 14:26 KJV*

> *"Hear, ye deaf; and look, ye blind, that ye may see. Who is blind, but my servant? or deaf, as my messenger that I sent? who is blind as he that is perfect, and blind as the Lord's servant? Seeing many things, but thou observest not; opening the ears, but he heareth not." Isaiah 42:18-20 KJV*

> *"Now when they had gone throughout Phrygia and the region of Galatia, and were forbidden of the Holy Ghost to preach the word in Asia, After they were come to Mysia, they assayed to go into Bithynia: but the Spirit suffered them not. And they passing by Mysia came down to Troas. And a vision appeared to Paul in the night; There stood a man of Macedonia, and prayed him, saying, Come over into Macedonia, and help us. And after he had seen the vision, immediately we endeavoured to go into Macedonia, assuredly gathering that the Lord had called us for to preach the gospel unto them." Acts 16:6-10 KJV*

2. Learn To Know God's Voice

The need to be sensitive to the Holy Spirit is for us to know when there is a shift in the spirit realm. Remember, we are not just spiritual, we are a spirit in a flesh, ably representing God here on earth. For us to be better representatives, we must be able to hear God's commands clearly and for this to be the case, we must know His voice. Jesus said "My sheep hear My voice…" If you are having trouble hearing His voice, you might need to check your status. Are you still a sheep? Does Jesus know you? Are you still following Him? If you are His sheep you must know His voice, and when you know His voice then you can hear it and follow Him. When we do not follow closely, our hearing becomes unreliable because of the distance between us.

> *"My sheep hear my voice, and I know them, and they follow me:" John 10:27 KJV*

> *"And when he putteth forth his own sheep, he goeth before them, and the sheep follow him: for they know his voice. And a stranger will they not follow, but will flee from him: for they know not the voice of strangers." John 10:4-5 KJV*

The story of little Samuel in the temple points our attention to three things that we must look at to learn how we can recognize the voice of God:

- **Study The Word**

Samuel was a young boy brought into the temple by his mother. He had been pledged to the Lord from conception and was raised in a house where both parents attend Shiloh regularly. He had a solid background of church activities but did not have an encounter with the Lord. In 1 Samuel 3, the Bible says that "Samuel did not YET know the Lord, neither was the WORD of the Lord YET revealed to him." The easiest way to know His voice is to be familiar with His Word. God is revealed from the written Word found in the Bible.

> *"Now Samuel did not yet know the Lord, neither was the word of the Lord yet revealed unto him." 1 Samuel 3:7 KJV*

- **Abide In The House Of God**

Samuel lived in the temple — where the presence of the Lord dwells — and so should we. Not by going to live in a church of course since the presence of God is everywhere. God is living inside of you! Every time we fellowship with other Christians is an opportunity to learn how to hear, recognize and obey that voice. The more you attend church, the better your hearing gets. The Lord called Samuel three times before he finally got it. The Lord is patient with us throughout the process and He's eager for us to get it so that He can fellowship with us on a personal level.

> *"And the Lord called Samuel again the third time. And he arose and went to Eli, and said, Here am I; for thou didst call me. And Eli perceived that the Lord had called the child." 1 Samuel 3:8 KJV*

- **Find Your Eli**

Samuel did not yet know the Lord, neither was the word of the Lord yet revealed unto him, but there was an ELI available to guide and direct him through the process.

Without an Eli in your life it might be difficult for you to understand the voice of the Lord and that might delay your progress and hinder you from being able to fully demonstrate your representative status. Who is your ELI? This could be your pastor, or a fellow Christian with a life full of fruits. It is your Eli that will guide and teach you what to say when God starts talking to you, so that when that voice comes again you will be ready, willing, and able to do what the voice tells you to do.

> *"Therefore Eli said unto Samuel, Go, lie down: and it shall be, if he call thee, that thou shalt say, Speak, Lord; for thy servant heareth. So Samuel went and lay down in his place." 1 Samuel 3:9 KJV*

APPLICATION

Now is the time to begin to apply these principles. When you look into the word of God for His voice, you abide in the house of the Lord, and you allow His presence to be carried with you. With Eli present in your life and gently guiding you through the process, you will finally master His voice. The Lord is patient with you throughout this process; His pleasure is for us to hear that still small voice from within.

> *"And the Lord came, and stood, and called as at other times, Samuel, Samuel. Then Samuel answered, Speak; for thy servant heareth." 1 Samuel 3:10 KJV*

Daniel got it. He had an excellent spirit by the virtue of his gifting, but without the ability to hear the voice of God, all his visions would have perished. His ability to hear made him a star in Babylon. On one particular occasion, he had a vision about the future and was seeking understanding and meaning of the vision, then he saw an appearance of a man but there was no interpretation. Then he heard the voice of the man that appeared to him, saying "Gabriel, make this man (Daniel) to understand the vision..." Until you know and hear the voice, you might not be able to represent Him well.

> *"And it came to pass, when I, even I Daniel, had seen the vision, and sought for the meaning, then, behold, there stood before me as the appearance of a man. And I heard a man's voice between the banks of Ulai, which called, and said, Gabriel, make this man to understand the vision." Daniel 8:15-16 KJV*

CHAPTER THREE

THE ENFORCER OF GOD'S WILL

God created man in His own image, desiring nothing but the best for His creation. He created man and deposited in him everything that He (God) is including all the power needed by man to subdues the earth and have dominion. God said unto man, be fruitful, and multiply, and replenish the earth, and SUBDUE IT, AND HAVE DOMINION over every created thing — what an influence He gave to man! From the sixth day man assumed the control of the entire creation — what an awesome privilege!

However, this great privilege was short lived and man lost the power to subdue and have dominion in the garden. The serpent took over from man and reduced the epic of God's creation to a powerless and fearful being.

The story of the man in Mark 5 who lived in the tomb with an unclean spirit depicts in essence humanity's deplorable state after the fall of man in Genesis 3. No one could tame him; nothing could soften the demonic influence on him — no chains or fetters; no therapy — day and night, he was in the mountains (surrounded by troubles on all sides), crying and cutting himself with stones (no rest whatsoever). This is the what man looked like after he fell in the garden, and so is a man without an indwelling presence of God. Man is absolutely powerless without God, but thanks to Jesus Who brought us back to our rightful place and gave us all power in heaven and on earth, restoring to man the power to subdue the earth and have dominion over it.

> *"So God created man in his own image, in the image of God created he him; male and female created he them. And God blessed them, and God said unto them, Be fruitful, and multiply, and replenish the earth, and subdue it: and have dominion over the fish of the sea, and over the fowl of the air, and over every living thing that moveth upon the earth." Genesis 1:27-28 KJV*

> *"When the unclean spirit is gone out of a man, he walketh through dry places, seeking rest, and findeth none. Then he saith, I will return into my house from whence I came out; and when he is come, he findeth it empty, swept, and garnished. Then goeth he, and taketh with himself seven other spirits more wicked than himself, and they enter in and dwell there: and the last state of that man is worse than the first. Even so shall it be also unto this wicked generation." Matthew 12:43-45 KJV*

> *"And when he was come out of the ship, immediately there met him out of the tombs a man with an unclean spirit, Who had his dwelling among the tombs; and no*

man could bind him, no, not with chains: Because that he had been often bound with fetters and chains, and the chains had been plucked asunder by him, and the fetters broken in pieces: neither could any man tame him. And always, night and day, he was in the mountains, and in the tombs, crying, and cutting himself with stones." Mark 5:2-5 KJV

"And when they were come to the multitude, there came to him a certain man, kneeling down to him, and saying, Lord, have mercy on my son: for he is lunatic, and sore vexed: for ofttimes he falleth into the fire, and oft into the water. And I brought him to thy disciples, and they could not cure him." Matthew 17:14-16 KJV

"And Jesus came and spake unto them, saying, All power is given unto me in heaven and in earth." Matthew 28:18 KJV

FOUR LEVELS OF ENFORCEMENT

Man's authority was restored by the finished work of grace done by Jesus Christ, and dominion over all the works of devil is now within reach. God has designated man as an enforcer of His will on earth. "Thy will be done on earth as it is in heaven." I have identified four levels of enforcement, viz: resisting the devil, tormenting the devil, casting out the devil and destroying the works of the devil. Let us discuss each one briefly.

1. Resisting The Devil

This is the first level of enforcement. It begins with our submission to God — you cannot resist the devil if you are not submitted to God. When we are fully yielded to the Word of God, the devil sees us as a threat. Telling him to get out of your way is as simple as shooting one verse from the Word. This level is for beginners in spiritual warfare. At this level, the devil accords you some respect but can still come to attack from time to time. This is like playing a tug of war with the devil.

"Submit yourselves therefore to God. Resist the devil, and he will flee from you." James 4:7 KJV

"And have no fellowship with the unfruitful works of darkness, but rather reprove them." Ephesians 5:11 KJV

2. Tormenting The Devil

The devil is afraid of believers who know their right and their standing in Jesus. They are the tormentors. Sure thing, the devil does not want to be tormented. He's like a bully that when subdued will always accord you respect from the moment you manifest your superiority over him. To resist the devil is good but to torment the devil is a show of power. Thus, when we understand that we are the sons of the most high God, we get it and the kingdom of darkness is in trouble.

"But when he saw Jesus afar off, he ran and worshipped him, And cried with a loud voice, and said, What have I to do with thee, Jesus, thou Son of the most high God? I adjure thee by God, that thou torment me not." Mark 5:6-7 KJV

3. Casting Out The Devil

The third level of enforcement entails creating a 'no parking' zone for the devil. On this level, the devil knows that you have a restraining order on him; he knows your level of your authority and knows that you will not hesitate to unleash your fury on him. To cast out suggests that the devil is not allowed to be in the same place with you. When you resist the devil, the devil may exchange words with you; when you torment the devil, the devil still wants to claim some right of occupancy for one reason or the other; but when you cast him out — like when Jesus suffered the demons not to speak — you don't allow the devil to exchange words with you because you are far above principalities and powers.

> *"And he healed many that were sick of divers diseases, and cast out many devils; and suffered not the devils to speak, because they knew him. And he preached in their synagogues throughout all Galilee, and cast out devils."*
> *Mark 1:34, 39 KJV*

4. Destroying The Works Of The Devil

This is the ultimate level of enforcement — destroying the works of the devil. For this purpose — to eliminate the works of the devil completely — Jesus the Son of God was manifested to destroy the works of the devil. He was manifested in us, because the earnest expectation of creation is waiting for you and I. As such, we have been anointed to destroy the devil's works and to deliver creation from the bondage of corruption into the glorious liberty of the children of God. It is high time we showed up and take our rightful position. It is good to resist the devil, even better to torment the devil, beautiful to cast the devil out, but the person the devil fears the most is the one who destroys his works. This is the class you belong to; you have all the power in heaven and on earth to do that.

> *"He that committeth sin is of the devil; for the devil sinneth from the beginning. For this purpose the Son of God was manifested, that he might destroy the works of the devil." 1 John 3:8 KJV*

> *"For the earnest expectation of the creature waiteth for the manifestation of the sons of God. For the creature was made subject to vanity, not willingly, but by reason of him who hath subjected the same in hope, Because the creature itself also shall be delivered from the bondage of corruption into the glorious liberty of the children of God. For we know that the whole creation groaneth and travaileth in pain together until now." Romans 8:19-22 KJV*

DAVID AND GOLIATH

To say that God was with David will be an understatement. David was a man after God's heart. He was renowned for bringing down one of the toughest enemies of the children of Israel — Goliath. Goliath must have ranked amongst the top three enemies the Israelites ever fought. David operated by divine revelation. In Psalms 86:6, it was revealed to him that we are gods. Goliath defied the army of the living God the same way the devil tries to challenge us in our everyday life, but David killed him with a stone — a shadow of the stone that was rejected by the builders

Who became the Chief Cornerstone — even Christ in us, our hope of glory. This same shadow found expression as the stone not cut by human hands and which broke into pieces the image seen by King Nebuchadnezzar in his dream. At the mention of the name of Jesus, every knee must bow!

> *"And the men of Israel said, Have ye seen this man that is come up? surely to defy Israel is he come up: and it shall be, that the man who killeth him, the king will enrich him with great riches, and will give him his daughter, and make his father's house free in Israel. And David spake to the men that stood by him, saying, What shall be done to the man that killeth this Philistine, and taketh away the reproach from Israel? for who is this uncircumcised Philistine, that he should defy the armies of the living God? And David put his hand in his bag, and took thence a stone, and slang it, and smote the Philistine in his forehead, that the stone sunk into his forehead; and he fell upon his face to the earth." 1 Samuel 17:25-26, 49 KJV*

> *"Thou sawest till that a stone was cut out without hands, which smote the image upon his feet that were of iron and clay, and brake them to pieces. Forasmuch as thou sawest that the stone was cut out of the mountain without hands, and that it brake in pieces the iron, the brass, the clay, the silver, and the gold; the great God hath made known to the king what shall come to pass hereafter: and the dream is certain, and the interpretation thereof sure." Daniel 2:34, 45 KJV*

SEVEN SONS OF SCEVA

God did many things with Paul and through him; he was a man of depth and revelation. He revealed the mystery of Christ in us as the hope of glory — a man well known in the spirit world. The sons of Sceva must have seen Paul in action while dealing with demons, sicknesses and performing special miracles — a man in whom God dwells. The Bible described the sons of Sceva as vagabond Jews — self-acclaimed exorcists; they had no relationship with Jesus. Paul on the other hand had the command of the spirit world, but not these guys. They went about trying to cast out demons in the name of Jesus whom Paul preached. The evil spirit challenged them with an all-important question: WHO ARE YOU? The spirit acknowledged their awareness of Paul and Jesus (and by implication, its subjection to the authority they carry). In other words, when you have God inside of you, you have an identity which the demonic world knows and that makes your territory a 'no go' zone. Good enough, God is no respecter of persons; whoever fears Him gets accepted into this elite armies of enforcers.

> *"And God wrought special miracles by the hands of Paul: So that from his body were brought unto the sick handkerchiefs or aprons, and the diseases departed from them, and the evil spirits went out of them. Then certain of the vagabond Jews, exorcists, took upon them to call over them which had evil spirits the name of the Lord Jesus, saying, We adjure you by Jesus whom Paul preacheth. And there were seven sons of one Sceva, a Jew, and chief of the priests, which did so. And the evil spirit answered and said, Jesus I know, and Paul I know;*

but who are ye? And the man in whom the evil spirit was leaped on them, and overcame them, and prevailed against them, so that they fled out of that house naked and wounded." Acts 19:11-16 KJV

"Then Peter opened his mouth, and said, Of a truth I perceive that God is no respecter of persons: But in every nation he that feareth him, and worketh righteousness, is accepted with him." Acts 10:34-35 KJV

HOW CAN I BECOME A BETTER ENFORCER?

1. Use The Name of Jesus Effectively

There is only one name that's effective in the spirit world, whether in heaven, on earth, or under the earth — the name of Jesus has jurisdiction in all these three realms. God has highly exalted Jesus and given Him a name. That name remains powerful throughout eternity! If indeed, as Jesus said, we will do greater works, then we need to leverage on the power in the name of Jesus. When the disciples came back from their exploits when they were sent out by Jesus, they testified, "Lord, even, the devils (or demons) are subject to us THROUGH YOUR NAME." Jesus's response was phenomenal; He said "I beheld satan as lightning falling from the heavenly places!" When you use the name of Jesus, the devil will always fall!

"Wherefore God also hath highly exalted him, and given him a name which is above every name: That at the name of Jesus every knee should bow, of things in heaven, and things in earth, and things under the earth; And that every tongue should confess that Jesus Christ is Lord,

to the glory of God the Father." Philippians 2:9-11 KJV

"And the seventy returned again with joy, saying, Lord, even the devils are subject unto us through thy name. And he said unto them, I beheld Satan as lightning fall from heaven. Behold, I give unto you power to tread on serpents and scorpions, and over all the power of the enemy: and nothing shall by any means hurt you." Luke 10:17-19 KJV

2. Use The Word Effectively

Jesus said it is impossible to go into a strong man's house (the devil) and spoil his goods without first binding the strong man with the word of God. He said that whatsoever we bind on earth is bound in heaven. We do this by the Word! David gave an insight as to what the Word of God can do: it can bring you into a great spoil! In a sense, David said "I rejoice at thy word, because it is the final authority in all human matters!" Jesus healed, and cast out evil spirits with His Word. He sent His word and it delivered (all of us) from what was meant to destroy us.

"Or else how can one enter into a strong man's house, and spoil his goods, except he first bind the strong man? and then he will spoil his house." Matthew 12:29 KJV

"I rejoice at thy word, as one that findeth great spoil." Psalms 119:162 KJV

"When the even was come, they brought unto him many that were possessed with devils: and he cast out the spirits with his word, and healed all that were sick:" Matthew 8:16 KJV

"He sent his word, and healed them, and delivered them from their destructions." Psalms 107:20 KJV

3. Tarry In Jerusalem

Jesus gave us an insight to the secret of being fully equipped with power for the journey ahead. The secret to getting divine power was for the Apostles to tarry in Jerusalem until they were endued with power. What a revelation! The Apostles tarried in Jerusalem for ten days and the unimaginable happened; the Holy Spirit came suddenly like a sound of a rushing mighty wind, the spirit appeared like cloven tongues of fire (a token that reminds us that the Holy Spirit will affect our tongue) and sat upon each of them (for the Holy Spirit will sit on a believer and take over from him/her) and they began to speak in tongues. It is of utmost importance that every single Christian follows this instruction, to tarry in the presence of God until (s)he is filled with the Holy Spirit, because that's the source of power for every conquest in the Christian race. The initial evidence of this infilling is speaking in tongues. Jesus cannot go wrong; you must be filled with the Holy Spirit — that's how divine secrets to deal with principalities, powers, and rulers of darkness are revealed. I pray that you will be filled with the Holy Spirit with the evidence of speaking in tongues.

"The secret things belong unto the Lord our God: but those things which are revealed belong unto us and to our children forever, that we may do all the words of this law." Deuteronomy 29:29 KJV

"And, behold, I send the promise of my Father upon you: but tarry ye in the city of Jerusalem, until ye be endued

with power from on high." Luke 24:49 KJV

"But ye shall receive power, after that the Holy Ghost is come upon you: and ye shall be witnesses unto me both in Jerusalem, and in all Judaea, and in Samaria, and unto the uttermost part of the earth." Acts 1:8 KJV

"And when the day of Pentecost was fully come, they were all with one accord in one place. And suddenly there came a sound from heaven as of a rushing mighty wind, and it filled all the house where they were sitting. And there appeared unto them cloven tongues like as of fire, and it sat upon each of them. And they were all filled with the Holy Ghost, and began to speak with other tongues, as the Spirit gave them utterance." Acts 2:1-4 KJV

CHAPTER FOUR

THE MOUTHPIECE OF GOD

God gave man dominion over the earth from the beginning. He made man His able representative in all affairs. We are His ambassadors with the full backing of heaven's authority to do as it pleases Him. With this privilege comes the opportunity to become the mouthpiece of God on earth.

God told Moses, "I will go with your mouth, and teach you what to say." God's will and pleasure is communicated through man; whenever He wants to say something, He does so through a man. This is why God is so particular about the use of our tongue. For God to speak through man (and by 'man', both genders are implied), He needs to dwell not with man but in man. This arrangement has made man a very important partner with God. God has to reveal His divine plan for humanity to man. God's secret is revealed to man in the flesh, and not to the angels.

There are many examples in the Bible of how God used

man as His mouthpiece, but I will make references to the two case studies Jesus mentioned: He said that as it was in the days of Noah, so shall the coming of the Son of man be and as Jonah was three days and three nights in the whale's belly, so shall the Son of man be three days and three nights in the heart of the earth. These two examples — Noah and Jonah — did what we are supposed to be doing as the mouthpiece of God, reaching out to the dying world.

God began to reveal His plan to Noah in Genesis 6. He was fed up with the corruption of man; their sins disgusted Him so much that He wanted to destroy everything that was created. What did God do? God found Himself a mouthpiece amongst men! He approached Noah and told him to build an ark for the salvation of man. Noah did according to all that God commanded him, and he began to tell others about the impending doom, but the people were given to eating and drinking until the judgement came, so Noah built an ark for the salvation of his family. As a mouthpiece of God, the salvation of Noah's household must be of utmost importance.

In like manner, God saw the lawlessness in Nineveh; as usual God employed Himself a mouthpiece and commanded Jonah to go and cry against the city in case the people will repent and be saved. Jonah eventually went after his initial disobedience, the people of Nineveh repented and the entire city was saved!

As a mouthpiece of God, our community and city is our responsibility — to evangelize for God therein. Jesus made mention of these two mouthpieces because one brought his family to God and the other, a city to God. Jesus so much believed in man as God's mouthpiece that He told everyone listening that everything written about Him in the law of Moses, and in the prophets, and in the book of Psalms must be fulfilled because the utterances were made by the mouthpieces of God speaking out the divine plan.

> *"And the Lord said unto him, Who hath made man's mouth? or who maketh the dumb, or deaf, or the seeing, or the blind? have not I the Lord? Now therefore go, and I will be with thy mouth, and teach thee what thou shalt say." Exodus 4:11-12 KJV*

> *"But as the days of Noah were, so shall also the coming of the Son of man be. For as in the days that were before the flood they were eating and drinking, marrying and giving in marriage, until the day that Noah entered into the ark, And knew not until the flood came, and took them all away; so shall also the coming of the Son of man be." Matthew 24:37-39 KJV*

> *"For as Jonas was three days and three nights in the whale's belly; so shall the Son of man be three days and three nights in the heart of the earth. The men of Nineveh shall rise in judgment with this generation, and shall condemn it: because they repented at the preaching of Jonas; and, behold, a greater than Jonas is here." Matthew 12:40-41 KJV*

> *"And he said unto them, These are the words which I spake unto you, while I was yet with you, that all things must be fulfilled, which were written in the law of Moses, and in the prophets, and in the psalms, concerning me." Luke 24:44 KJV*

AARON, THE MOUTH FOR MOSES

God speaks, and since we are made in the image and the likeness of God, He gave us the same ability and as long as we are alive, God expects us to continually speak. He has chosen us to be His mouthpiece, to communicate His wishes on earth. When God called Moses to go on an assignment of delivering the children of Israel from the land of Egypt, he responded and told God about his speech impediment — as if God did not know he had it. Moses lost the opportunity to be the mouthpiece of God though he was a good friend of God. God appointed Aaron his brother as the mouthpiece in his stead. The lesson for us here is that God expects everyone of us to be His mouthpiece, but if we don't embrace the responsibility, He can delegate it to someone else. I think this is the main reason why Christians likes to seek after prophets or prophecy because they have decided that they did not want to hear or speak for God.

> *"And he shall be thy spokesman unto the people: and he shall be, even he shall be to thee instead of a mouth, and thou shalt be to him instead of God." Exodus 4:16 KJV*

> *"And the Lord said unto Moses, See, I have made thee a god to Pharaoh: and Aaron thy brother shall be thy prophet." Exodus 7:1 KJV*

ELIJAH THE PROPHET

Our relationship with God gets better with time. The more time we spend with Him, the more we get to know Him. As with every relationship where intimacy is growing, there comes a point where you can almost certainly predict the behavioral pattern of whom you are in a relationship with; the same is true with God. Of course, no one can figure God out because He's ways above us, but when we get to know and abide by His will, when we say anything, heaven backs it up.

As a mouthpiece of God, Elijah went to the messengers of king Ahaziah after he directed them to seek counsel from a pagan god, he told them to go back to the king and tell him that he would die of his injuries. The king was very upset about the verdict that he sent armies to go and get Elijah, but the prophet invoked his right as a mouthpiece of God and said "If I BE A MAN OF GOD, let fire come down and consume these armies…" God must have looked at him and said, "Sure, he's my man and everything that comes out of his mouth, I am obliged to back up because he's in line with my agenda." Of course, this is not to say that we have the power to curse whosoever we don't like, no. Elijah was in tune with God, as such his words are more-or-less God's words.

At another instance, Elijah said to king Ahab (who was notorious for disobedience), "At my word, there shall be no rain until I say so." In this instance, it is unlikely that God instructed him to say that, but since he shared God's dislike for the lifestyle of these people, God had to back up his words. God defends anything a man that is His mouthpiece says. The lesson for us is to spend time with God, so that we can move from being a mouthpiece to becoming such a person who speaks for God and whose words God backs up.

> *"Then the king sent unto him a captain of fifty with his fifty. And he went up to him: and, behold, he sat on the*

top of an hill. And he spake unto him, Thou man of God, the king hath said, Come down. And Elijah answered and said to the captain of fifty, If I be a man of God, then let fire come down from heaven, and consume thee and thy fifty. And there came down fire from heaven, and consumed him and his fifty. Again also he sent unto him another captain of fifty with his fifty. And he answered and said unto him, O man of God, thus hath the king said, Come down quickly. And Elijah answered and said unto them, If I be a man of God, let fire come down from heaven, and consume thee and thy fifty. And the fire of God came down from heaven, and consumed him and his fifty. And he sent again a captain of the third fifty with his fifty. And the third captain of fifty went up, and came and fell on his knees before Elijah, and besought him, and said unto him, O man of God, I pray thee, let my life, and the life of these fifty thy servants, be precious in thy sight." 2 Kings 1:9-13 KJV

"And Elijah the Tishbite, who was of the inhabitants of Gilead, said unto Ahab, As the Lord God of Israel liveth, before whom I stand, there shall not be dew nor rain these years, but according to my word." 1 Kings 17:1 KJV

ELISHA THE PROPHET

A mouth piece is someone that provides divine direction to others. It's such a great privilege and honor. This is what Elisha did in the passage below. Imagine the president of France, United States, and Britain, coming to you for direction on a national or global matter — that's what happens when you become the mouthpiece of God. My father in the Lord, Bishop David Oyedepo has always said that God is raising giants on our platform that will take the world by storm! Global mouthpieces of God. A time is coming that the world will look to the church for guidance because committed Christians will have access to divine information, because all the springs that will make the world function well are domicile in Zion. As a mouthpiece of God, we are to live up to our status as a peculiar people seated with christ in heavenly places.

> *"And the king of Israel said, Alas! that the Lord hath called these three kings together, to deliver them into the hand of Moab! But Jehoshaphat said, Is there not here a prophet of the Lord, that we may enquire of the Lord by him? And one of the king of Israel's servants answered and said, Here is Elisha the son of Shaphat, which poured water on the hands of Elijah. And Jehoshaphat said, The word of the Lord is with him. So the king of Israel and Jehoshaphat and the king of Edom went down to him. And Elisha said unto the king of Israel, What have I to do with thee? get thee to the prophets of thy father, and to the prophets of thy mother. And the king of Israel said unto him, Nay: for the Lord hath called these three kings together, to deliver them into the hand of Moab. And Elisha said, As the Lord of hosts liveth, before whom I stand, surely, were it not that I regard the presence of Jehoshaphat the king of Judah, I would not look toward thee, nor see thee. But now bring me a minstrel. And it came to pass, when the minstrel played, that the hand of the Lord came upon him. And he said, Thus saith the Lord, Make this valley full of ditches. For thus saith the Lord, Ye shall not see wind, neither shall*

ye see rain; yet that valley shall be filled with water, that ye may drink, both ye, and your cattle, and your beasts." 2 Kings 3:10-17 KJV

JOHN THE BAPTIST

John was the forerunner of Jesus Christ who bore witness of Him, saying "He that comes after me is preferred above me, for He was before me." He was a mouthpiece who spoke concerning Jesus and he also baptized Him. John's event in the new testament was already foretold by another mouthpiece of God, prophet Isaiah, who said that there is "a voice of him who cries in the wilderness, saying prepare ye the way of the Lord, make straight in the desert a highway for our God." It happened just as prophesied. Now we have a better understanding why Jesus said that everything in the Law of Moses, in the prophets and in the book of Psalms must be fulfilled about Him. By implication and application, the lesson for us here is to also look throughout the Bible and make sure that everything that has been written therein concerning us be fulfilled in our lives. I want to challenge you to look for at least ten promises in the Bible and put your stake in the hole until those promises manifest in your life.

"The voice of him that crieth in the wilderness, Prepare ye the way of the Lord, make straight in the desert a highway for our God. Every valley shall be exalted, and every mountain and hill shall be made low: and the crooked shall be made straight, and the rough places plain: And the glory of the Lord shall be revealed, and all flesh shall see it together: for the mouth of the Lord hath spoken it. The voice said, Cry. And he said, What

shall I cry? All flesh is grass, and all the goodliness thereof is as the flower of the field: The grass withereth, the flower fadeth: because the spirit of the Lord bloweth upon it: surely the people is grass. The grass withereth, the flower fadeth: but the word of our God shall stand for ever." Isaiah 40:3-8 KJV

"John bare witness of him, and cried, saying, This was he of whom I spake, He that cometh after me is preferred before me: for he was before me. And of his fullness have all we received, and grace for grace. For the law was given by Moses, but grace and truth came by Jesus Christ. No man hath seen God at any time; the only begotten Son, which is in the bosom of the Father, he hath declared him. And this is the record of John, when the Jews sent priests and Levites from Jerusalem to ask him, Who art thou? He said, I am the voice of one crying in the wilderness, Make straight the way of the Lord, as said the prophet Esaias." John 1:15-19, 23 KJV

HOW DO I BECOME A BETTER MOUTHPIECE

1. Use Your Tongue Wisely

A man who wants be a mouthpiece of God must have a total control on the use of the tongue. The tongue is a little member in the body but can cause the most problem. God is looking for people with wholesome tongues to reveal and release His divine counsel for this generation to them. Death and life are in the power of the tongue; let us use it wisely! It is one of the qualities that God is looking for in us before He can commit anything tangible to our hands.

"Even so the tongue is a little member, and boasteth great things. Behold, how great a matter a little fire kindleth! And the tongue is a fire, a world of iniquity: so is the tongue among our members, that it defileth the whole body, and setteth on fire the course of nature; and it is set on fire of hell. For every kind of beasts, and of birds, and of serpents, and of things in the sea, is tamed, and hath been tamed of mankind: But the tongue can no man tame; it is an unruly evil, full of deadly poison." James 3:5-8 KJV

"Death and life are in the power of the tongue: and they that love it shall eat the fruit thereof." Proverbs 18:21 KJV

2. Say What God Says

If we want to be an effective mouthpiece of God, then we must say what God says. The sign of any true prophet is to see what he says come to pass. If that doesn't happen, then such a man is a false prophet or faulty mouthpiece. How can we begin to say what God says? By hiding the word of God in our hearts! David said "Your word l have hidden in my heart, that l might not sin against you." If we do not sin with our tongues, we are regarded as being perfect. Since we are the redeemed of the Lord, the Bible says "let the redeemed of the Lord say so" — say what the Lord is saying. Finally as God's mouthpieces, we can count on His promise to give us a mouth and wisdom, which all our adversaries shall not be able to gainsay nor resist.

"Let the redeemed of the Lord say so, whom he hath redeemed from the hand of the enemy;" Psalms 107:2 KJV

"Thy word have I hid in mine heart, that I might not sin against thee." Psalms 119:11 KJV

"For I will give you a mouth and wisdom, which all your adversaries shall not be able to gainsay nor resist." Luke 21:15 KJV

3. Be Filled With The Holy Spirit

The Spirit of God is the only One that knows the things of God. So the Holy Spirit is the custodian of all the mysteries of the kingdom including the plan and purpose for us. An effective mouthpiece must therefore be filled with the Holy Spirit for him/her to know the mind of God concerning any issue. The ministry of the Holy Spirit is so vital that Jesus said l will pray to the father to send the comforter and His last instructions to His disciples was for them to stay in Jerusalem until that Holy Spirit is received from the Father. The Holy Spirit will make any man from any background an effective mouthpiece, so endeavor to be filled with Him; He will change everything — even your prayer life.

"For what man knoweth the things of a man, save the spirit of man which is in him? even so the things of God knoweth no man, but the Spirit of God. Now we have received, not the spirit of the world, but the spirit which is of God; that we might know the things that are freely given to us of God." 1 Corinthians 2:11-12 KJV

"And I will pray the Father, and he shall give you another Comforter, that he may abide with you forever; But the Comforter, which is the Holy Ghost, whom the Father will send in my name, he shall teach you all

things, and bring all things to your remembrance, whatsoever I have said unto you." John 14:16, 26 KJV

4. Desire The Gifts of The Spirit

Paul was speaking to the Corinthians about spiritual gifts in 1 Corinthians 12. He said he did not want them to be ignorant about the giftings of the Holy Spirit. It is very possible to be filled with the Holy Spirit and not know all the benefits He brings. The Holy Spirit has gifts and fruits that make the Christian walk of any believer even better. There are three categories of the gifts of the Holy Spirit, viz: gifts of revelation (mind gifts), gifts of inspiration (vocal gifts) and gifts of power (working gifts). All these gifts are needed to be an effective mouthpiece for God. Desire earnestly these gifts to be in manifestation in your life since the Holy Spirit is giving these gifts to every man severally as He wills — and it is the will of God for us to have the gifts in order to carry out an effective ministry.

"Now concerning spiritual gifts, brethren, I would not have you ignorant. But the manifestation of the Spirit is given to every man to profit withal. For to one is given by the Spirit the word of wisdom; to another the word of knowledge by the same Spirit; To another faith by the same Spirit; to another the gifts of healing by the same Spirit; To another the working of miracles; to another prophecy; to another discerning of spirits; to another divers kinds of tongues; to another the interpretation of tongues: But all these worketh that one and the selfsame Spirit, dividing to every man severally as he will." 1 Corinthians 12:1, 7-11 KJV

CHAPTER FIVE

THE COMMANDER OF GOD'S ARMY

God made man in His image and likeness and that comes with various privileges. King David expressed the magnitude of glory that man enjoys by being made in God's image when he said "You have made man a little lower than Elohim, and crowned him with glory and honor, and has made him to have dominion over the works of His hand and has put ALL THINGS under his feet." Beloved, it is very difficult to wrap our mind around this, because it is quite unbelievable that the creator of the whole universe will entrust man with so much! He has put everything under our feet — and that includes all the angelic host, every animal, the storm, wind, hurricane, tsunami, water, fire — just to mention a few. And you wonder why the devil is very jealous of you?

God never said to any angel, "sit at my right hand until I make your enemies your footstool"; He said that only to Jesus, and Jesus is domicile in us. Besides, angels are ministering spirits sent forth to minister to us who are now heirs of salvation. All these give us full command; angels are at our call and command. Abraham lived out this reality when he took total control of the situation regarding what would eventually happen in Sodom and Gomorrah. Three angels appeared to Abraham and began to tell him about their mission to Sodom and Gomorrah — how their iniquities has come up to God and He has ordered them to be destroyed. I believe the reason why the angels engaged him in the discussion was for him to tell them what to do. God has put all things under our feet! Abraham had the power that day to call off that devastation and he did try but stopped too soon. If Abraham had negotiated down to only one righteous man, imagine what would have happened.

We are the commander of the entire heaven's army! What we say goes; we are the shot callers — that's how far God has elevated us. If we look at the example of Gideon, after the angel visited him, he asked the angel to do certain things which the angel gladly obliged. We are the commander of everything God created. It's no wonder David could kill the the bear and the lion with his hand; Daniel could outlive a night in the lion's den and the three Hebrew boys in the fiery furnace came out the fire untouched. Jesus rebuked the storm and wind, in fact all the miracles He did, He did them all while in the flesh. It is high time we assumed our rightful place in the hierarchy of heavenly command, so that we can enjoy our inheritance in Christ Jesus.

> *"For thou hast made him a little lower than the angels, and hast crowned him with glory and honour. Thou madest him to have dominion over the works of thy*

hands; thou hast put all things under his feet:" Psalms 8:5-6 KJV

"And of the angels he saith, Who maketh his angels spirits, and his ministers a flame of fire. But unto the Son he saith, Thy throne, O God, is for ever and ever: a sceptre of righteousness is the sceptre of thy kingdom. But to which of the angels said he at any time, Sit on my right hand, until I make thine enemies thy footstool? Are they not all ministering spirits, sent forth to minister for them who shall be heirs of salvation?" Hebrews 1:7-8, 13-14 KJV

"And the Lord appeared unto him in the plains of Mamre: and he sat in the tent door in the heat of the day; And he lift up his eyes and looked, and, lo, three men stood by him: and when he saw them, he ran to meet them from the tent door, and bowed himself toward the ground, And the men rose up from thence, and looked toward Sodom: and Abraham went with them to bring them on the way. And the Lord said, Shall I hide from Abraham that thing which I do; Peradventure there shall lack five of the fifty righteous: wilt thou destroy all the city for lack of five? And he said, If I find there forty and five, I will not destroy it. And he spake unto him yet again, and said, Peradventure there shall be forty found there. And he said, I will not do it for forty's sake. And he said unto him, Oh let not the Lord be angry, and I will speak: Peradventure there shall thirty be found there. And he said, I will not do it, if I find thirty there. And he said, Behold now, I have taken upon me to speak unto the Lord: Peradventure there shall be twenty found there. And he said, I will not destroy it for twenty's sake. And he said, Oh let not the

Lord be angry, and I will speak yet but this once: Peradventure ten shall be found there. And he said, I will not destroy it for ten's sake. And the Lord went his way, as soon as he had left communing with Abraham: and Abraham returned unto his place." Genesis 18:1-2, 16-17, 28-33 KJV

MOSES COMMANDED THE RED SEA

God created man and put him in control of everything. When Moses led the Israelites to the Red Sea, he asked God for what to do. God asked him "why are you crying to me?" He told Moses to divide the sea and indeed, the sea did not part until Moses took his rightful place as a commander over that body of water. The answer was in Moses' mouth all along. "Speak to the children of Israel to go forward!" A commander commands. When Moses commanded the sea, the people went on a dry land. God has delegated all authority to us as the field commanders. He is the same yesterday, today and forever. His sea-splitting power — physically or spiritually — is still alive!

"And the Lord said unto Moses, Wherefore criest thou unto me? speak unto the children of Israel, that they go forward: But lift thou up thy rod, and stretch out thine hand over the sea, and divide it: and the children of Israel shall go on dry ground through the midst of the sea. And it came between the camp of the Egyptians and the camp of Israel; and it was a cloud and darkness to them, but it gave light by night to these: so that the one came not near the other all the night. And Moses stretched out his hand over the sea; and the Lord caused the sea to go back by a strong east wind all that night,

and made the sea dry land, and the waters were divided. And the children of Israel went into the midst of the sea upon the dry ground: and the waters were a wall unto them on their right hand, and on their left." Exodus 14:15-16, 20-22 KJV

JOSHUA COMMANDED THE SUN AND MOON

When God speaks, everything listens! That's how He created the all of creation — He spoke all things into being. Joshua lived out this reality of having command over all creation when he told the sun and moon to stand still and they both obeyed his command. The problem we have today is that we underestimate the power that lies within us. We need to always remember that God is domicile in us and that everything bows at His command. God has honored man's command many times over in the scriptures. Hezekiah asked Isaiah what will be the proof that he will be cured from his illness, and the proof he got was God turning back the sun by ten degrees — what an awesome power! It is hard to believe but if you will only dare to believe, the sun and the moon will yield to your command; you are that powerful!

"And it came to pass, as they fled from before Israel, and were in the going down to Beth–horon, that the Lord cast down great stones from heaven upon them unto Azekah, and they died: they were more which died with hailstones than they whom the children of Israel slew with the sword. Then spake Joshua to the Lord in the day when the Lord delivered up the Amorites before the children of Israel, and he said in the sight of Israel, Sun,

stand thou still upon Gibeon; and thou, Moon, in the valley of Aijalon. And the sun stood still, and the moon stayed, until the people had avenged themselves upon their enemies. Is not this written in the book of Jasher? So the sun stood still in the midst of heaven, and hasted not to go down about a whole day. And there was no day like that before it or after it, that the Lord hearkened unto the voice of a man: for the Lord fought for Israel." Joshua 10:11-14 KJV

"And this shall be a sign unto thee from the Lord, that the Lord will do this thing that he hath spoken; Behold, I will bring again the shadow of the degrees, which is gone down in the sun dial of Ahaz, ten degrees backward. So the sun returned ten degrees, by which degrees it was gone down." Isaiah 38:7-8 KJV

ELISHA COMMANDS THE BEAR

Elijah and Elisha are two men that demonstrated the power of God in ordinary men beyond any doubt. Elijah, the spiritual father of Elisha, called down fire from heaven to fight his perceived enemies and his spiritual son called a bear to attack his mockers. I was wondering why the bear did not attack Elisha — such wild animals could hardly differentiate the children from the prophet — but it goes to show that Elisha was in full command. Yes, we even have command over dangerous animals. Of course, I am not advocating that you go out and endanger your life, but if you ever found yourself in a situation whereby a dangerous animal is trying to attack you, it is within your command to stay its power.

"And he went up from thence unto Beth–el: and as he was going up by the way, there came forth little children out of the city, and mocked him, and said unto him, Go up, thou bald head; go up, thou bald head. And he turned back, and looked on them, and cursed them in the name of the Lord. And there came forth two she bears out of the wood, and tare forty and two children of them." 2 Kings 2:23-24 KJV

JESUS COMMANDED FOOD TO MULTIPLY

God spoke to the ground to bring forth herbs as food for man, and the earth brought out plenty. Elijah went to the widow who was about to die due to the famine in the land, he commanded the cruse of oil and the barrel of wheat to continue to supply for three and half years, and it was so! Yes, food obeys our command. Jesus blessed the lunch of a little boy and it fed five thousand men without counting women and children. It might sound funny but you are a food commander! As a commander of God's army, every creation — living or not — bows at your command. Step up and take charge and control of everything that surrounds your life.

"But Jesus said unto them, They need not depart; give ye them to eat. And they say unto him, We have here but five loaves, and two fishes. He said, Bring them hither to me. And he commanded the multitude to sit down on the grass, and took the five loaves, and the two fishes, and looking up to heaven, he blessed, and brake, and gave the loaves to his disciples, and the disciples to the multitude. And they did all eat, and were filled:

and they took up of the fragments that remained twelve baskets full. And they that had eaten were about five thousand men, beside women and children." Matthew 14:16-21 KJV

HOW DO I BECOME A BETTER COMMANDER?

1. You Are Greater Than The Greatest.

The new testament Christian has so much power beyond any measure of comparison. If we are to look at the old testament, we can easily point to God's men that were endowed with His power — many actually. The good news is that Jesus came to the world as a man and identified with us. He said that among those that are born of women — including Moses, Elijah, Elisha, Joshua, and many of the prophets — there has not risen a man greater than John the Baptist. But He goes on to say that — and this is the part that excites me more — NOTWITHSTANDING, he that is LEAST in the kingdom of heaven is greater than he (John the Baptist). It is unquantifiable the amount of power in us! We are greater in every measure through Jesus Christ.

"Verily I say unto you, Among them that are born of women there hath not risen a greater than John the Baptist: notwithstanding he that is least in the kingdom of heaven is greater than he. And from the days of John the Baptist until now the kingdom of heaven suffereth violence, and the violent take it by force." Matthew 11:11-12 KJV

2. See Yourself In Your Position.

What makes us greater than the greatest in the world? It is our position in Christ. We have been raised from the dead with Jesus and God has made us to sit with Christ in heavenly places far above all principalities, power, might, and dominion. This position allows us to have total command over everything. He has put ALL THINGS under our feet.

> *"Which he wrought in Christ, when he raised him from the dead, and set him at his own right hand in the heavenly places, Far above all principality, and power, and might, and dominion, and every name that is named, not only in this world, but also in that which is to come: And hath put all things under his feet, and gave him to be the head over all things to the church, Which is his body, the fullness of him that filleth all in all." Ephesians 1:20-23 KJV*

3. Know Your Right.

Knowing our right is the first thing that gives us command and control over all creation. If any man be in Christ, he is a new creation and sin can no longer stop such a person from his/her rights. Through Jesus, we have a right standing with God. He has made us righteous by His own standard. The seed of God remains in us, and because of that seed, it is impossible to remain a sinner. This is what gives us mastery over all of creation.

> *"Therefore if any man be in Christ, he is a new creature: old things are passed away; behold, all things are become new. For he hath made him to be sin for us, who knew*

no sin; that we might be made the righteousness of God in him." 2 Corinthians 5:17, 21 KJV

"Whosoever is born of God doth not commit sin; for his seed remaineth in him: and he cannot sin, because he is born of God." 1 John 3:9 KJV

CHAPTER SIX

THE EPITOME OF GOD'S POWER

God's power is very real. This is why David said that God's people shall be willing in the day of His power. The good news is that God's power is available everyday to anyone willing to tap into it. We saw the power at work from the beginning — the earth was without form, and void and darkness was upon the face of the deep. Yet, in all of these emptiness, the creative power of God began to manifest. For us to attempt to know the magnitude of this power — and we can only attempt — we need to examine the different manifestations of the power.

1 Kings 19:11-12 helped us divide the manifestations of divine power into four parts:

1. A Great and Strong Wind
2. An Earthquake
3. Fire (with smoke everywhere) and
4. A Still Small Voice.

God's power has been demonstrated in all these dimensions at one time or the other in the Bible. Let us consider a few examples.

Moses brought forth the people out of the camp to meet with God, and the people stood afar off. The Lord descended and there was smoke everywhere because the Lord has descended on the mountain in the form of fire. The smoke thereof ascended and there was an earthquake all round. Another example was when the ark of covenant was brought to River Jordan. As soon as the priests bearing the ark stepped into the water, the water separated and the children of Israel walked to the other side on a dry land. Joshua did not have to say a word; the water bowed to the power in the chest. The power of God manifested again on the Mount of Transfiguration. Jesus was transformed by the power of God in a manner that was so real that Peter, James and John heard the thundering thereof and they bowed in awe until Jesus touched them. This awesome power has been deposited in man, and was visibly displayed while God was dwelling with man and even more so now that He dwells in man.

> *"Thy people shall be willing in the day of thy power, in the beauties of holiness from the womb of the morning: thou hast the dew of thy youth." Psalms 110:3 KJV*

> *"And the earth was without form, and void; and darkness was upon the face of the deep. And the Spirit of God moved upon the face of the waters." Genesis 1:2 KJV*

> *"And he said, Go forth, and stand upon the mount before the Lord. And, behold, the Lord passed by, and*

a great and strong wind rent the mountains, and brake in pieces the rocks before the Lord; but the Lord was not in the wind: and after the wind an earthquake; but the Lord was not in the earthquake: And after the earthquake a fire; but the Lord was not in the fire: and after the fire a still small voice." 1 Kings 19:11-12 KJV

"And Moses brought forth the people out of the camp to meet with God; and they stood at the nether part of the mount. And mount Sinai was altogether on a smoke, because the Lord descended upon it in fire: and the smoke thereof ascended as the smoke of a furnace, and the whole mount quaked greatly. And when the voice of the trumpet sounded long, and waxed louder and louder, Moses spake, and God answered him by a voice." Exodus 19:17-19 KJV

"And thou shalt command the priests that bear the ark of the covenant, saying, When ye are come to the brink of the water of Jordan, ye shall stand still in Jordan. And it shall come to pass, as soon as the soles of the feet of the priests that bear the ark of the Lord, the Lord of all the earth, shall rest in the waters of Jordan, that the waters of Jordan shall be cut off from the waters that come down from above; and they shall stand upon an heap. And it came to pass, when the people removed from their tents, to pass over Jordan, and the priests bearing the ark of the covenant before the people; And as they that bare the ark were come unto Jordan, and the feet of the priests that bare the ark were dipped in the brim of the water, (for Jordan overfloweth all his banks all the time of harvest,) That the waters which came down from above stood and rose up upon an heap very far from the city Adam, that is beside Zarethan:

and those that came down toward the sea of the plain, even the salt sea, failed, and were cut off: and the people passed over right against Jericho. And the priests that bare the ark of the covenant of the Lord stood firm on dry ground in the midst of Jordan, and all the Israelites passed over on dry ground, until all the people were passed clean over Jordan." Joshua 3:8, 13-17 KJV

"And was transfigured before them: and his face did shine as the sun, and his raiment was white as the light. And, behold, there appeared unto them Moses and Elias talking with him." Matthew 17:2-3 KJV

MOSES WITH THE VEIL

God frequently visited with men, and when He does, His power and presence is felt all over the earth. Moses had many encounters with God. It was said that he was very meek and that God speaks with him face to face. During one of his encounters with God, the children of Israel could not look at his face because of the radiating power from his face. He had to put on a veil to talk with the people. That was an evidence of God's power dwelling with man — the power was real, palpable and very visible (most of the time).

"And it came to pass, when Moses came down from mount Sinai with the two tables of testimony in Moses' hand, when he came down from the mount, that Moses wist not that the skin of his face shone while he talked with him. And when Aaron and all the children of Israel saw Moses, behold, the skin of his face shone; and they were afraid to come nigh him. And Moses called unto

them; and Aaron and all the rulers of the congregation returned unto him: and Moses talked with them. And afterward all the children of Israel came nigh: and he gave them in commandment all that the Lord had spoken with him in mount Sinai. And till Moses had done speaking with them, he put a veil on his face. But when Moses went in before the Lord to speak with him, he took the veil off, until he came out. And he came out, and spake unto the children of Israel that which he was commanded. And the children of Israel saw the face of Moses, that the skin of Moses' face shone: and Moses put the veil upon his face again, until he went in to speak with him." Exodus 34:29-35 KJV

FROM ELIJAH TO ELISHA

Prophet Elijah was one of God's men. He was a man full of confidence with a track record of numerous encounters with the visible power of God. Prophet Elijah called down power from heaven to consume bands of army that came to arrest him; he commanded it not rain for three and a half years; he was fed by the raven and he supplied a widow and her kid with food throughout the period of drought in Samaria. All these are the manifestations of the power of God. But that was not all… Elijah also had the grace to impart and transfer the power on him to his spiritual protégé, Elisha. Elijah asked Elisha for what he wanted from him and having seen his mentor's several accomplishments, he asked for the double portion of his spirit. God has given him the grace to transfer what was upon him to Elisha. Elisha waited and followed Elijah patiently until the chariot of fire from heaven came down and Elisha got his wish; he was endowed with the double portion of Elijah's power when the mantle fell from Elijah.

> *"And it came to pass, when they were gone over, that Elijah said unto Elisha, Ask what I shall do for thee, before I be taken away from thee. And Elisha said, I pray thee, let a double portion of thy spirit be upon me. And he said, Thou hast asked a hard thing: nevertheless, if thou see me when I am taken from thee, it shall be so unto thee; but if not, it shall not be so. And it came to pass, as they still went on, and talked, that, behold, there appeared a chariot of fire, and horses of fire, and parted them both asunder; and Elijah went up by a whirlwind into heaven." 2 Kings 2:9-11 KJV*

THE BONES OF ELISHA

Prophet Elisha got double portion of prophet Elijah's power. There are fourteen powerful manifestations in Elijah's ministry as recorded in the Bible and Elisha had double of those to his record — twenty eight. Indeed, he got it. The last of Elisha's miracles did not happen in his life time, though. He was dead and buried — we don't know for how long — but the power of God was still stored up in his dead bones such that when a dead man was thrown into his grave, the dead man came back alive when his dead body touched the dead bone of Elisha. The power of God was still active in a dead bone! Imagine what that power will do in the life of a born again child of God?

> *"And Elisha died, and they buried him. And the bands of the Moabites invaded the land at the coming in of the year. And it came to pass, as they were burying a*

man, that, behold, they spied a band of men; and they cast the man into the sepulchre of Elisha: and when the man was let down, and touched the bones of Elisha, he revived, and stood up on his feet." 2 Kings 13:20-21 KJV

PETER'S SHADOW

God is the same yesterday, today and forever. The power of God was displayed all over the old testaments in divers manifestations — real, visible and palpable power. Then Jesus came and died for us to bring us back to the original plan of God dwelling in man with all His power as evident in the old testament. We saw in many instances the demonstrations of God's power in the ministry of Jesus and even more after the Holy Spirit came on the scene. Jesus instructed the disciples to stay in Jerusalem until they were endued with power from above. The evidence of that power was visible in the ministry of the Apostles. Peter demonstrated that power in a very unusual way according to Luke's account in the book of Acts when he said that Peter's shadow healed the sick and dealt with the unclean spirits so much so that multitude brought their sick families and laid them on the streets. This power is real and available to us today — the capacity of a born again child of God is unquantifiable!

"Insomuch that they brought forth the sick into the streets, and laid them on beds and couches, that at the least the shadow of Peter passing by might overshadow some of them. There came also a multitude out of the cities roundabout unto Jerusalem, bringing sick folks, and them which were vexed with unclean spirits: and they were healed everyone." Acts 5:15-16 KJV

HOW DO I BECOME MORE ENDOWED WITH POWER?

1. The Power of The Word

God upholds all things by the Word of His power. The Word of God is very powerful; it is creative in nature. The same Word created the entire earth in six days; delivered Jesus from temptations in the wilderness and casted out demons. With Jesus' three it-is-writtens, the devil left Him and an angel ministered to Him. The more of the Word of God we have in us, the greater the power for in the beginning was the Word, and the Word was with God and the Word was God.

> *"Who being the brightness of his glory, and the express image of his person, and upholding all things by the word of his power, when he had by himself purged our sins, sat down on the right hand of the Majesty on high;" Hebrews 1:3 KJV*

> *"But he answered and said, It is written, Man shall not live by bread alone, but by every word that proceedeth out of the mouth of God. Jesus said unto him, It is written again, Thou shalt not tempt the Lord thy God. Then saith Jesus unto him, Get thee hence, Satan: for it is written, Thou shalt worship the Lord thy God, and him only shalt thou serve. Then the devil leaveth him, and, behold, angels came and ministered unto him." Matthew 4:4, 7, 10-11 KJV*

> *"When the even was come, they brought unto him many that were possessed with devils: and he cast out the spirits with his word, and healed all that were sick:" Matthew 8:16 KJV*

2. Effectual Fervent Prayer

The effectual fervent prayer of a righteous man makes the power of God available. If Jesus has become our righteousness, then every single prayer that we pray must generate tremendous amount of power. Paul gave us few examples of how to pray for God's power to be activated from within us. In his prayer for the Ephesian church, Paul gave thanks and asked for the spirit of wisdom and revelation of Jesus Christ — that our eyes of understanding of the heavenly mysteries be enlightened, that we may understand the hope of His calling, and the depth of the riches of His inheritance in the saint, so that we can experience the greatness of His power. Another example of this prayer is found in Ephesians 3:16-20.

> *"That he would grant you, according to the riches of his glory, to be strengthened with might by his Spirit in the inner man; That Christ may dwell in your hearts by faith; that ye, being rooted and grounded in love, May be able to comprehend with all saints what is the breadth, and length, and depth, and height; And to know the love of Christ, which passeth knowledge, that ye might be filled with all the fullness of God. Now unto him that is able to do exceeding abundantly above all that we ask or think, according to the power that worketh in us." Ephesians 3:16-20 KJV*

> *"Confess your faults one to another, and pray one for another, that ye may be healed. The effectual fervent prayer of a righteous man availeth much." James 5:16 KJV*

"Cease not to give thanks for you, making mention of you in my prayers; That the God of our Lord Jesus Christ, the Father of glory, may give unto you the spirit of wisdom and revelation in the knowledge of him: The eyes of your understanding being enlightened; that ye may know what is the hope of his calling, and what the riches of the glory of his inheritance in the saints, And what is the exceeding greatness of his power to us-ward who believe, according to the working of his mighty power." Ephesians 1:16-19 KJV

3. The Mantle's Phenomenon

The power of God is transferable from one point to the other. We saw that in the old testament with the pillars of cloud and fire in the wilderness, likewise with the presence of the ark of covenant. The ark of covenant carried so much power that it defeated enemies and defended itself when confiscated by enemy nations. Again, when the mantle fell from Elijah to Elisha, the power of God was transferred. In the new testament, we read about the shadow of Peter healing the sick and special miracles by the hands of Paul such that from his body were brought handkerchiefs (mantle) that healed the sick. The power of God is transferable and that, till today.

"And it came to pass, as they still went on, and talked, that, behold, there appeared a chariot of fire, and horses of fire, and parted them both asunder; and Elijah went up by a whirlwind into heaven. And Elisha saw it, and he cried, My father, my father, the chariot of Israel, and the horsemen thereof. And he saw him no more: and he took hold of his own clothes, and rent them in two pieces.

He took up also the mantle of Elijah that fell from him, and went back, and stood by the bank of Jordan;" 2 Kings 2:11-13 KJV

"And he commanded the most mighty men that were in his army to bind Shadrach, Meshach, and Abed–nego, and to cast them into the burning fiery furnace. Then these men were bound in their coats, their hosen, and their hats, and their other garments, and were cast into the midst of the burning fiery furnace. Therefore because the king's commandment was urgent, and the furnace exceeding hot, the flame of the fire slew those men that took up Shadrach, Meshach, and Abed–nego." Daniel 3:20-22 KJV

"And God wrought special miracles by the hands of Paul: So that from his body were brought unto the sick handkerchiefs or aprons, and the diseases departed from them, and the evil spirits went out of them." Acts 19:11-12 KJV

4. Faith Without Works Is Dead

Without faith it is impossible to please God. Faith is needed in all our transactions with God. Faith moves mountains. James, however, talks about faith without works being dead. In other words, faith alone is dead. Juxtaposing this with what Jesus said in John 14:12 where He talks about us doing greater works, it becomes clear that without faith, we cannot do any work. Many Christians are expecting to see the manifestations of God's power in their lives and even want to do greater works, yet they will not attempt to pray for the sick. Faith without works is believing that God can heal the sick but not responding to the prompting to pray for a co-worker or a fellow Christian about their needs. When Peter and John saw a crippled man at the beautiful gate, not only did they pray but also pulled the man up and told him to rise up and walk. For us to see the manifestations of God's power we must add work to our faith.

> *"Even so faith, if it hath not works, is dead, being alone. Yea, a man may say, Thou hast faith, and I have works: shew me thy faith without thy works, and I will shew thee my faith by my works. Thou believest that there is one God; thou doest well: the devils also believe, and tremble. But wilt thou know, O vain man, that faith without works is dead?" James 2:17-20 KJV*

> *"Verily, verily, I say unto you, He that believeth on me, the works that I do shall he do also; and greater works than these shall he do; because I go unto my Father." John 14:12 KJV*

> *"Then Peter said, Silver and gold have I none; but such as I have give I thee: In the name of Jesus Christ of Nazareth rise up and walk. And he took him by the right hand, and lifted him up: and immediately his feet and ankle bones received strength. And he leaping up stood, and walked, and entered with them into the temple, walking, and leaping, and praising God." Acts 3:6-8 KJV*

CHAPTER SEVEN

THE CUSTODIAN OF ALL GOD'S RESOURCES

On the sixth day, God created man and blessed them. He said to them, "Be fruitful, and multiply, and replenish the earth, and subdue it, and have dominion." This five-fold blessing brought man into total control of all of God's resources. Everything God created was officially transferred to come under man's dominion and each dimension of this blessing truly reveals the potential of any man. So man can be fruitful, can multiply and replenish on demand. Man was never created to fail because God can never fail.

HOW WEALTHY IS GOD?

God's wealth can never be quantified its dimensions unsearchable. Psalm 24:1-2 reveals to us that the earth is the Lord's and the fullness thereof; the world and everything that occupies it belongs to God. Humans live on just one of the many planets in the universe — and they all belong to Him. All the resources on earth — mineral, financial, agricultural, atmospheric, and supernatural resources — all the money in the world — they all belong to God. He said that the desire of all nations shall come for both the silver and gold belongs to Him. He declared that every beast of the forest is His — including the cattle upon a thousand hills. Who can put a value on all these? Now, imagine what it should be like for this vast God to live in a man — how could such a man be broke? David understood this revelation when he said "I have been young and now old, I have not seen a righteous forsaken or his seed begging for bread." The value of a man in whom God dwells is so much that when the devil was successful in deceiving man, God committed His best asset to ensuring the redemption of man back to Himself. The loss of man became unbearable for God in whom He had so much investment.

"And God blessed them, and God said unto them, Be fruitful, and multiply, and replenish the earth, and subdue it: and have dominion over the fish of the sea, and over the fowl of the air, and over every living thing that moveth upon the earth." Genesis 1:28 KJV

"The earth is the Lord's, and the fulness thereof; the world, and they that dwell therein. For he hath founded it upon the seas, and established it upon the floods." Psalms 24:1-2 KJV

"And I will shake all nations, and the desire of all nations shall come: and I will fill this house with glory, saith the Lord of hosts. The silver is mine, and the gold is mine, saith the Lord of hosts." Haggai 2:7-8 KJV

"For every beast of the forest is mine, and the cattle upon a thousand hills. I know all the fowls of the mountains: and the wild beasts of the field are mine." Psalms 50:10-11 KJV

"I have been young, and now am old; yet have I not seen the righteous forsaken, nor his seed begging bread." Psalms 37:25 KJV

THE FIVE CARDINAL BLESSINGS ON MAN

Let us look at these five cardinal blessings that make man the custodian of God's resources.

1. Be Fruitful

God commanded man to be fruitful because He expected man to be a god with creative powers — being made in the image and after the likeness of God. The fruit-bearing capability is what gives us our identity. We are supposed to produce fruit after the kind that God produces! Jesus was so particular about man's ability to bear fruits that He said "any man who wants to bear fruits like God must abide in Him." He said that every tree that does not produce the God-kind of fruit is to be cut down and cast into fire.

"Ye shall know them by their fruits. Do men gather grapes of thorns, or figs of thistles? Even so every good tree bringeth forth good fruit; but a corrupt tree bringeth forth evil fruit. A good tree cannot bring forth evil fruit, neither can a corrupt tree bring forth good fruit. Every tree that bringeth not forth good fruit is hewn down,

and cast into the fire. Wherefore by their fruits ye shall know them." Matthew 7:16-20 KJV

2. Multiply

The multiplication capabilities of God was very evident at creation. On the first day, He said let there be light and there was light and the light multiplied till light became available everywhere on the earth. On the second day, He created the heavens and multiple heavens appeared — hence Paul's reference to 'third heavens'. On the third day of creation, dry land (called earth) was created. Again, multiple lands with different terrains came up and brought forth multiple grasses and herbs. On the fourth day, He created multiple seasons, signs, stars... and the fifth day welcomed multiple kinds of animals in their multitudes. On the sixth day, He created man with the power to multiply and to perform as a god.

The Lord reminded Abram of his ability to multiply like Him; He took him outside to look at the heavens and count the stars in order to reacquaint Abram with His ability, not only to bring about fruitfulness, but also to divinely multiply. Jesus demonstrated this ability to multiply when He multiplied two fish and five loaves of bread. Every child of God has the same capacity within him or her.

"And, behold, the word of the Lord came unto him, saying, This shall not be thine heir; but he that shall come forth out of thine own bowels shall be thine heir. And he brought him forth abroad, and said, Look now toward heaven, and tell the stars, if thou be able to number them: and he said unto him, So shall thy seed be." Genesis 15:4-5 KJV

"The Lord your God hath multiplied you, and, behold, ye are this day as the stars of heaven for multitude. (The Lord God of your fathers make you a thousand times so many more as ye are, and bless you, as he hath promised you!)" Deuteronomy 1:10-11 KJV

3. Replenish The Earth

God revealed something powerful to us about His ability to replenish or revitalize the earth. We understand that the earth was not created on the third day — the land was, and it was renamed the earth. But a closer look at Genesis 1:2 suggests that the earth was already in existence. It was without form and void, and darkness was upon the face of the deep. But God is a specialist in rebranding and replenishing — and what He did with the formless void earth, He has given us the blessing to do. He commissioned Noah to function in this replenishing dimension when He destroyed the earth with water. He asked him to build an ark for that purpose, with divine instructions on how to do it. We have this power to replenish anything in us because this awesome God dwells within us.

"In the beginning God created the heaven and the earth. And the earth was without form, and void; and darkness was upon the face of the deep. And the Spirit of God moved upon the face of the waters." Genesis 1:1-2 KJV

"And it repented the Lord that he had made man on the earth, and it grieved him at his heart. And the Lord said, I will destroy man whom I have created from the face of the earth; both man, and beast, and the creeping thing, and the fowls of the air; for it repenteth me that I have made them. But Noah found grace in the eyes of

the Lord. Make thee an ark of gopher wood; rooms shalt thou make in the ark, and shalt pitch it within and without with pitch." Genesis 6:6-8, 14 KJV

4. Subdue The Earth

The earth is God's footstool — everything therein is subjected to Him. God transferred this power to Adam in the garden of Eden. All of creation is subject to God — the moon, sun, rain...every living and non-living thing; when He speaks, everything responds — this is why Jesus said that if the people refuse to praise Him, He would command the stones to praise Him. Joshua, Isaiah and Elisha — to mention a few — demonstrated the ability of man to subdue the earth — a man in whom God dwells has this ability at his disposal.

"Thus saith the Lord, The heaven is my throne, and the earth is my footstool: where is the house that ye build unto me? and where is the place of my rest?" Isaiah 66:1 KJV

"The Lord by wisdom hath founded the earth; by understanding hath he established the heavens. By his knowledge the depths are broken up, and the clouds drop down the dew." Proverbs 3:19-20 KJV

"The Lord said unto my Lord, Sit thou at my right hand, until I make thine enemies thy footstool." Psalms 110:1 KJV

5. Dominion Over The Earth

It will be an understatement to say that God has power over the earth. The heaven is His throne and the earth

His footstool. His power and splendor is well demonstrated in His creation and they are in total submission to Him. However, He rested from all His work on the seventh day and transferred all the power and dominion to man to reign upon the earth, and commanded him to have dominion over the earth. Man lost this due to sin in the garden but thankfully Christ Jesus regained it for us.

> *"For the earnest expectation of the creature waiteth for the manifestation of the sons of God. For the creature was made subject to vanity, not willingly, but by reason of him who hath subjected the same in hope, Because the creature itself also shall be delivered from the bondage of corruption into the glorious liberty of the children of God. For we know that the whole creation groaneth and travaileth in pain together until now." Romans 8:19-22*

ABRAHAM, THE COVENANT MAN

God was very fond of Abraham and expressed all the five cardinal blessings in his life. Abraham literarily lived by every command from the Lord. The Lord asked him to leave his people and go to the land that will be revealed to him. He obeyed God all the way and as a result an everlasting covenant was built on his obedience. Now we joyfully refer to God as the God of Abraham, Isaac and Jacob — He has become our God through Jesus; all the blessings lost have now been recovered based on the obedience of Jesus.

> *"And the angel of the Lord called unto Abraham out of heaven the second time, And said, By myself have I sworn, saith the Lord, for because thou hast done this thing, and hast not withheld thy son, thine only son:*

That in blessing I will bless thee, and in multiplying I will multiply thy seed as the stars of the heaven, and as the sand which is upon the sea shore; and thy seed shall possess the gate of his enemies; And in thy seed shall all the nations of the earth be blessed; because thou hast obeyed my voice." Genesis 22:15-18 KJV

SOLOMON ASKED FOR WISDOM

In the wisdom of God lies all the provision of God. The five cardinal blessings on man is accessible through Wisdom. Solomon the son of David of the lineage of Abraham the friend of God, asked for this wisdom and he got it. As believers in the finished works of Christ, we have access to the same because in us dwells the Son of David — Jesus, the wisdom and power of God.

"In Gibeon the Lord appeared to Solomon in a dream by night: and God said, Ask what I shall give thee. And God said unto him, Because thou hast asked this thing, and hast not asked for thyself long life; neither hast asked riches for thyself, nor hast asked the life of thine enemies; but hast asked for thyself understanding to discern judgment; Behold, I have done according to thy words: lo, I have given thee a wise and an understanding heart; so that there was none like thee before thee, neither after thee shall any arise like unto thee. And I have also given thee that which thou hast not asked, both riches, and honour: so that there shall not be any among the kings like unto thee all thy days." 1 Kings 3:5, 11-13 KJV

HOW CAN I BECOME A BETTER CUSTODIAN?

1. Know What You Have In Christ

It is imperative for us to know what we have in Christ — what has been freely given to us. God who has decided to dwell in man comes with all the resources that makes Him God — what a wealthy place we now find ourselves! Jesus is the firstborn among the brethren and has made us a joint-heir with Him. With that arrangement, we have now become a chosen generation and a royal priesthood with total access to all of God's resources.

> *"The Spirit itself beareth witness with our spirit, that we are the children of God: And if children, then heirs; heirs of God, and joint-heirs with Christ; if so be that we suffer with him, that we may be also glorified together." Romans 8:16-17 KJV*

> *"But ye are a chosen generation, a royal priesthood, an holy nation, a peculiar people; that ye should shew forth the praises of him who hath called you out of darkness into his marvellous light: Which in time past were not a people, but are now the people of God: which had not obtained mercy, but now have obtained mercy." 1 Peter 2:9-10 KJV*

2. Have Respect For The Covenant

God has always operated on covenant practices. David asked God in Psalms 74:20 to have respect for the covenant He has made with His people. The problem with keeping covenant, however, is not with God but with us. In the areas of financial blessing, there are established covenant practices that are not debatable. God asked us to bring all the tithe to the store for a windfall of blessings, and to honor the Lord with our substance. God's too faithful to fail. He bound Himself with an oath to His Word. When we have respect for the covenant, God will reciprocate our obedience. If you want access to all the five cardinal blessings in Jesus, do whatsoever He tells you.

> *"Have respect unto the covenant: for the dark places of the earth are full of the habitations of cruelty." Psalms 74:20 KJV*

> *"While the earth remaineth, seedtime and harvest, and cold and heat, and summer and winter, and day and night shall not cease." Genesis 8:22 KJV*

3. Take Care of The Widow, Fatherless and Poor

There are three categories of people that move the heart of God: the widow, the fatherless and the poor. God knows that there will always be the poor among us; He provides for them through His people. When we do what moves His heart, God's hand is opened to us. The Bible says that God opens His hand and fulfill the desire of every living thing. God commanded the children of Israel not to harvest everything on their field and to leave some wheat on purpose so that the poor wouldn't have to beg to meet their needs.

> *"Blessed is he that considereth the poor: the Lord will deliver him in time of trouble. The Lord will preserve him, and keep him alive; and he shall be blessed upon the earth: and thou wilt not deliver him unto the will*

of his enemies. The Lord will strengthen him upon the bed of languishing: thou wilt make all his bed in his sickness." Psalms 41:1-3 KJV

"And when ye reap the harvest of your land, thou shalt not make clean riddance of the corners of thy field when thou reapest, neither shalt thou gather any gleaning of thy harvest: thou shalt leave them unto the poor, and to the stranger: I am the Lord your God." Leviticus 23:22 KJV

CHAPTER EIGHT

THE CLOSER OF GOD'S PLAN

God is so fond of man that He will not even close the chapter of history on this side of eternity until every man have had the opportunity to hear the gospel and decide where to spend eternity. Jesus asked a powerful question that really revealed how much God wants to dwell in us and not just with us besides unveiling the time table of the events of the end time. He said "What man of you, having hundred sheep and loses one will go and find it?" The answer was equally profound; He said that for the sake of ONE MAN, He will leave ninety nine that have received eternal life and go after that one — the lost one.

Man is at the center of God's plan having been made a little lower than ELOHIM. God has always depended on man to carry out His agenda and giving man the privilege to determine the closure of the final plan of God. God is always looking for man to stand in the gap as a savior, because until the gospel is preached to all men, the end will not come. Obadiah 1:21 tells us that saviors shall come up on Mount Zion. While Jesus is the only Savior, God does refer to any man that will engage in and advance His salvation agenda as saviors.

The simple responsibility of a savior is to save people from death whether eternally or temporarily and God has called us to both via the ministry of reconciliation. God's plan for us found full expression in the One we call the Son Of Man, Jesus Christ. He had to come as a man by holy conception and was born through the normal channel everyone of us came through. He came and declared His mission immediately — that the Son of Man has come to seek and save that which was lost. He began the work of the closure of God's plan and committed it to the hands of able men (His disciples), then to Paul for the gentiles and now we are responsible for the propagation of the gospel so that God can call all of us home. We are ambassadors of this mission.

> *"What man of you, having an hundred sheep, if he lose one of them, doth not leave the ninety and nine in the wilderness, and go after that which is lost, until he find it? And when he hath found it, he layeth it on his shoulders, rejoicing. And when he cometh home, he calleth together his friends and neighbours, saying unto them, Rejoice with me; for I have found my sheep which was lost. I say unto you, that likewise joy shall be in heaven over one sinner that repenteth, more than over ninety and nine just persons, which need no repentance. Either what woman having ten pieces of silver, if she lose one piece, doth not light a candle, and sweep the house, and seek diligently till she find it? And when she hath found it, she calleth her friends and her neighbours*

together, saying, Rejoice with me; for I have found the piece which I had lost. Likewise, I say unto you, there is joy in the presence of the angels of God over one sinner that repenteth." Luke 15:4-10 KJV

"And I sought for a man among them, that should make up the hedge, and stand in the gap before me for the land, that I should not destroy it: but I found none." Ezekiel 22:30 KJV

"And saviours shall come up on mount Zion to judge the mount of Esau; and the kingdom shall be the Lord's." Obadiah 1:21 KJV

"And this gospel of the kingdom shall be preached in all the world for a witness unto all nations; and then shall the end come." Matthew 24:14 KJV

"For the Son of man is come to seek and to save that which was lost." Luke 19:10 KJV

JOSEPH IN THE LAND OF EGYPT

Joseph had a dream that will lead him to a cascade of events according to God's plan for him to be one of the saviors of the chosen people of God through a story that teaches many lessons to us unto whom the end has come, so that we can prepare ourselves as saviors for this generation. Joseph went to the dungeon, to slavery and to the prison on his way to becoming a savior that will deliver an entire generation from death by hunger. We are saviors like Joseph to deliver this generation from the famine of the Word and to turn the famine to an hunger for God. We have been empowered (like Pharaoh empowered

Joseph) by the Holy Spirit to accomplish the task before us. The end will not come until everyone hears.

> *"And Joseph said unto his brethren, Come near to me, I pray you. And they came near. And he said, I am Joseph your brother, whom ye sold into Egypt. Now therefore be not grieved, nor angry with yourselves, that ye sold me hither: for God did send me before you to preserve life. For these two years hath the famine been in the land: and yet there are five years, in the which there shall neither be earing nor harvest. And God sent me before you to preserve you a posterity in the earth, and to save your lives by a great deliverance. So now it was not you that sent me hither, but God: and he hath made me a father to Pharaoh, and lord of all his house, and a ruler throughout all the land of Egypt." Genesis 45:4-8 KJV*

DANIEL AND HIS BROTHERS IN BABYLON

Daniel and his brothers were an example to Babylon. They refused to eat what others ate in the palace at Babylon in the days of their preparation. They looked different, never conforming to the world around them. They refused to obey an ungodly order to bow to an idol even to the extent of passing through the fiery furnace knowing fully well that God was preparing them as saviors for the people of Babylon. When the order of the king was urgent demanding to kill all the magicians and astrologers of the land with Daniel and his friends, Daniel came with the solution that saved the lives of many that day — what a savior! Shadrach, Meshach, and Abednego refused the order to bow. It looked like the end had come but they stood with the God of the Hebrew as the only God to be worshipped. In following their examples, we must not eat what the world eats, look like them or follow their norms so that we can be an effective savior as God has called us to be. We must not disappoint God, knowing that the end will not come if we are slack concerning this mandate.

> *"For this cause the king was angry and very furious, and commanded to destroy all the wise men of Babylon. And the decree went forth that the wise men should be slain; and they sought Daniel and his fellows to be slain. I thank thee, and praise thee, O thou God of my fathers, who hast given me wisdom and might, and hast made known unto me now what we desired of thee: for thou hast now made known unto us the king's matter. Therefore Daniel went in unto Arioch, whom the king had ordained to destroy the wise men of Babylon: he went and said thus unto him; Destroy not the wise men of Babylon: bring me in before the king, and I will shew unto the king the interpretation. Then Arioch brought in Daniel before the king in haste, and said thus unto him, I have found a man of the captives of Judah, that will make known unto the king the interpretation." Daniel 2:12-13, 23-25 KJV*

> *"Shadrach, Meshach, and Abed–nego, answered and said to the king, O Nebuchadnezzar, we are not careful to answer thee in this matter. If it be so, our God whom we serve is able to deliver us from the burning fiery furnace, and he will deliver us out of thine hand, O king. But if not, be it known unto thee, O king, that we will not serve thy gods, nor worship the golden image which thou hast set up. Then Nebuchadnezzar spake,*

and said, Blessed be the God of Shadrach, Meshach, and Abed–nego, who hath sent his angel, and delivered his servants that trusted in him, and have changed the king's word, and yielded their bodies, that they might not serve nor worship any god, except their own God. Therefore I make a decree, That every people, nation, and language, which speak anything amiss against the God of Shadrach, Meshach, and Abed–nego, shall be cut in pieces, and their houses shall be made a dunghill: because there is no other God that can deliver after this sort. Then the king promoted Shadrach, Meshach, and Abed–nego, in the province of Babylon." Daniel 3:16-18, 28-30 KJV

MORDECAI AND ESTHER BABYLON

The letter had been written by Haman to exterminate the entire Jewish race and the order has been sealed by the king's ring with no way out until saviors like Esther and Mordecai surfaced. They cried about the injustice of the letter, complained about it, and eventually sprung into action. They delivered the entire Jewish race and vengeance was executed upon their enemies. So also the devil and his cohorts have written a letter to destroy us, our children, families, businesses, careers, and most importantly our relationship with God. Like Esther and Mordecai, we must rise up to the occasion in fasting and prayers for this generation. Our complaints and lack of action will not stop the devil; we are saviors for this generation and we must destroy the letter of the devil in our societies, schools, families, businesses, children and in our churches. The spirit of Haman must be exterminated.

"And when Haman saw that Mordecai bowed not, nor

did him reverence, then was Haman full of wrath. And he thought scorn to lay hands on Mordecai alone; for they had shewed him the people of Mordecai: wherefore Haman sought to destroy all the Jews that were throughout the whole kingdom of Ahasuerus, even the people of Mordecai. If it please the king, let it be written that they may be destroyed: and I will pay ten thousand talents of silver to the hands of those that have the charge of the business, to bring it into the king's treasuries. And the king took his ring from his hand, and gave it unto Haman the son of Hammedatha the Agagite, the Jews' enemy." Esther 3:5-6, 9-10 KJV

"Then Esther bade them return Mordecai this answer, Go, gather together all the Jews that are present in Shushan, and fast ye for me, and neither eat nor drink three days, night or day: I also and my maidens will fast likewise; and so will I go in unto the king, which is not according to the law: and if I perish, I perish. So Mordecai went his way, and did according to all that Esther had commanded him." Esther 4:15-17 KJV

PETER IN JERUSALEM

Peter was a fisherman that was not capable of doing much. Yet, when Jesus was leaving, He committed everything to Peter's hand. Thinking about his arguments with Jesus, the denials before the rooster crowed, and how he abandoned the flock the moment Jesus was captured, he felt like a failure unable to accomplish the task. He didn't look like someone that could be called a savior — until that Pentecost morning. Something happened in the upper room that morning that changed Peter's story forever and he became a great soul harvester. You might think you are not capable, and have done things that disqualify you but in actual fact, you are the one God is looking for — the one to close out His plan here on earth. You shall receive power after the Holy Spirit has come upon you. The Spirit is available and as the psalmist said, God's people shall be willing in the days of His power. Get ready, set and go! Be that savior God has called you to be.

> *"He saith unto him the third time, Simon, son of Jonas, lovest thou me? Peter was grieved because he said unto him the third time, Lovest thou me? And he said unto him, Lord, thou knowest all things; thou knowest that I love thee. Jesus saith unto him, Feed my sheep." John 21:17 KJV*

"But Peter, standing up with the eleven, lifted up his voice, and said unto them, Ye men of Judaea, and all ye that dwell at Jerusalem, be this known unto you, and hearken to my words:

> *Then they that gladly received his word were baptized: and the same day there were added unto them about three thousand souls. And they continued steadfastly in the apostles' doctrine and fellowship, and in breaking of bread, and in prayers." Acts 2:14, 41-42 KJV*

HOW DO I BECOME A BETTER CLOSER OF GOD'S PLAN?

1. Pray For All Men

Paul had so much success in his ministerial efforts as a savior to the gentiles. He did so many things for the kingdom as a man of deep revelation and insight into the plan of God. He was well respected by other disciples and mostly revered by the authorities of his days. He gave us an inclination as to how he was able to procure so much success in his ministry. How did he do it? 1 Timothy 2:1 gives us a hint: "l exhort therefore, that first of all…" He's about to tell us the primary assignment of anyone who wants to be an effective savior — "to supplicate, pray, intercede and to give thanks for ALL MEN…" For us to see the plan of God of the gospel being preached to whole world, prayer is indispensable, more so for a man in whom God dwells. We are to pray for kings (the head of businesses, households, literal kings, etc) and those in authority at all levels — locally, regionally, statewide, nationally and on a global scale. This act of prayer and travailing is not only good but acceptable in the sight of God, our ULTIMATE SAVIOR, who will have ALL MEN to be saved and come to the knowledge of the truth.

"I exhort therefore, that, first of all, supplications, prayers, intercessions, and giving of thanks, be made for all men; For kings, and for all that are in authority; that we may lead a quiet and peaceable life in all godliness and honesty. For this is good and acceptable in the sight of God our Saviour; Who will have all men to be saved, and to come unto the knowledge of the truth." 1 Timothy 2:1-4 KJV

"My little children, of whom I travail in birth again until Christ be formed in you." Galatians 4:19 KJV

"Who hath heard such a thing? who hath seen such things? Shall the earth be made to bring forth in one day? or shall a nation be born at once? for as soon as

Zion travailed, she brought forth her children." Isaiah 66:8 KJV

2. Go After All Men

Jesus said that the Son of Man is come to seek and to save that which was lost. If we were to create a mission statement for Jesus' ministry, it will be "TO SEEK AND SAVE THE LOST." He advocated for it, prepared the disciples in training, sent them out two by two, empowered them for the work ahead with the ability to heal the sick and deliver the oppressed. He also said that greater works than he did has He empowered us to do; we are to start where He stopped — to turn many to righteousness. Indeed, it is a privilege to be part of this end time army because the harvest is plenty but the laborers are few. Let us therefore seek first the kingdom of God by going after souls and every other things shall be added unto us.

"After these things the Lord appointed other seventy also, and sent them two and two before his face into every city and place, whither he himself would come. Therefore said he unto them, The harvest truly is great, but the labourers are few: pray ye therefore the Lord of the harvest, that he would send forth labourers into his harvest." Luke 10:1-2 KJV

"And they that be wise shall shine as the brightness of the firmament; and they that turn many to righteousness as the stars for ever and ever." Daniel 12:3 KJV

"The fruit of the righteous is a tree of life; and he that winneth souls is wise." Proverbs 11:30 KJV

3. Do Good To All Men

Jesus declared that no one is good when He was addressed as a 'Good Master' by the rich young ruler. If no one is good, then how can we do good? John 14:26 enlightens us. There, Jesus said that it was expedient for Him to leave so that the Holy Spirit can be released to come to us. The Bible revealed to us in Acts 10:38 how God anointed Jesus of Nazareth with the Holy Ghost and power, who went about doing good. In other words, we can only afford to do good after the endowment and empowerment of the Holy Spirit. When the Holy Spirit empowers us, it can also be written of us — and of the saviors of these days — "How God anointed Joseph of El Paso, Texas, with the Holy Ghost and power: who went about doing good, and healing all that were oppressed of the devil; for God is with him." When we take care of the poor, the fatherless and the widows as highlighted in Matthew 25, then we are engaged in doing good and as a result we will see souls responding to our call for salvation. Isaiah 61 tells us what the anointing can do in any life. It will also make us the priests and ministers of our God. Start doing good and you will see how more people will respond to the gospel of Jesus Christ.

"And, behold, one came and said unto him, Good Master, what good thing shall I do, that I may have eternal life?

> *Jesus said unto him, If thou wilt be perfect, go and sell that thou hast, and give to the poor, and thou shalt have treasure in heaven: and come and follow me." Matthew 19:16, 21 KJV*

"How God anointed Jesus of Nazareth with the Holy Ghost and with power: who went about doing good, and healing all that were oppressed of the devil; for God was with him." Acts 10:38 KJV

"Trust in the Lord, and do good; so shalt thou dwell in the land, and verily thou shalt be fed." Psalms 37:3 KJV

"The Spirit of the Lord God is upon me; because the Lord hath anointed me to preach good tidings unto the meek; he hath sent me to bind up the brokenhearted, to proclaim liberty to the captives, and the opening of the prison to them that are bound; To proclaim the acceptable year of the Lord, and the day of vengeance of our God; to comfort all that mourn; To appoint unto them that mourn in Zion, to give unto them beauty for ashes, the oil of joy for mourning, the garment of praise for the spirit of heaviness; that they might be called trees of righteousness, the planting of the Lord, that he might be glorified. And they shall build the old wastes, they shall raise up the former desolations, and they shall repair the waste cities, the desolations of many generations. And strangers shall stand and feed your flocks, and the sons of the alien shall be your plowmen and your vinedressers. But ye shall be named the Priests of the Lord: men shall call you the Ministers of our God: ye shall eat the riches of the Gentiles, and in their glory shall ye boast yourselves." Isaiah 61:1-6 KJV

CHAPTER NINE

THE EPITOME OF GOD'S CREATION

Man is the epitome of God's creation. He was created last on the sixth day after which God rested from all His work on the seventh day. When God created everything from the first day to the fifth day, He said that they were good but when He created man, He said it was VERY GOOD. God considered us the best part of His creation, created in His image and likeness, male and female created He them and subjected every other creation under man's control and command. He created us with FREE WILL thereby making us so independent that we can choose to obey or disobey Him. God was not intimidated by us, not threatened by the authority and latitude He gave us. God so wanted man to be in total control that He entered into His rest on the seventh day, telling man to eat freely of the fruit of the garden and to stay away from the tree of the knowledge of good and evil, but man out of his free will chose to do otherwise and disobeyed. The disobedience continue into many generations and became so entrenched into the people that Joshua had to declare that as for him and his house, they will serve the Lord.

God created us with a free will to do as we please. He gave us so much latitude that He called the heaven and earth as a witness, so that when we make our decision whether to follow Him or not, there will be an evidence of His liberality with us. God said to the man He made without any coercion as it were, "I have set before you life and death, blessing and cursing..." He then advises us to choose life so that we can live. Jesus came to the world not to take away the free will of man but to further enhance our liberty in God. Even He was rejected by His own people. He did not force anyone to do anything — that's how much free will and power man got from His Creator, God.

Paul said that we have been called into liberty, but only not to use that liberty as an opportunity to disobey God because the Holy Spirit Who now dwells in us is the Spirit of liberty — where that Spirit exists, there is liberty! So with this much power, influence and free will, we need to remember that God is still supreme and high above all things. The discussion that follows is about eight things that keeps me humble and submitted to God, so that I do not take my liberty in Christ for granted, but rather to enlarge it.

"And God said, Let us make man in our image, after our likeness: and let them have dominion over the fish of the sea, and over the fowl of the air, and over the cattle, and over all the earth, and over every creeping thing that creepeth upon the earth. So God created man in his own image, in the image of God created he him; male and female created he them.

And God saw everything that he had made, and, behold, it was very good. And the evening and the morning were the sixth day." Genesis 1:26-27, 31 KJV

"And the Lord God commanded the man, saying, Of every tree of the garden thou mayest freely eat: But of the tree of the knowledge of good and evil, thou shalt not eat of it: for in the day that thou eatest thereof thou shalt surely die." Genesis 2:16-17 KJV

"And if it seem evil unto you to serve the Lord, choose you this day whom ye will serve; whether the gods which your fathers served that were on the other side of the flood, or the gods of the Amorites, in whose land ye dwell: but as for me and my house, we will serve the Lord." Joshua 24:15 KJV

"I call heaven and earth to record this day against you, that I have set before you life and death, blessing and cursing: therefore choose life, that both thou and thy seed may live: That thou mayest love the Lord thy God, and that thou mayest obey his voice, and that thou mayest cleave unto him: for he is thy life, and the length of thy days: that thou mayest dwell in the land which the Lord sware unto thy fathers, to Abraham, to Isaac, and to Jacob, to give them." Deuteronomy 30:19-20 KJV

"For, brethren, ye have been called unto liberty; only use not liberty for an occasion to the flesh, but by love serve one another." Galatians 5:13 KJV

"Now the Lord is that Spirit: and where the Spirit of

the Lord is, there is liberty. But we all, with open face beholding as in a glass the glory of the Lord, are changed into the same image from glory to glory, even as by the Spirit of the Lord." 2 Corinthians 3:17-18 KJV

8 SUBMISSION POINTS FOR MAN

These are eight reminders I give myself to grant myself perspective — that I am still subject to God.

1. I am just a witness.

In the court of law anywhere in the world, you have these three characters: the judge, the prosecutor and the defendant. It has never been documented anywhere in the world that a witness was declared the winner of any lawsuit because a witness is just a witness even though (s)he can be an essential and integral part of the case. In like manner, man was made in the image and likeness of God — which, in a sense, makes man a little god — but still, he is just a witness and can never take credit for any happenings in his or her universe. Therefore let us strive to be an effective witness so that we can be found worthy as a co-laborer in God's vineyard. Man is not the light; he cannot see far without the real light in him. He will be useless and ready for the trash can without the light of God which is the life of God in man.

"The same came for a witness, to bear witness of the Light, that all men through him might believe. He was not that Light, but was sent to bear witness of that Light. That was the true Light, which lighteth every man that cometh into the world. He was in the world, and the

world was made by him, and the world knew him not. He came unto his own, and his own received him not." John 1:7-11 KJV

"But ye shall receive power, after that the Holy Ghost is come upon you: and ye shall be witnesses unto me both in Jerusalem, and in all Judaea, and in Samaria, and unto the uttermost part of the earth." Acts 1:8 KJV

2. I am a co-laborer, a sub-contractor and a hired laborer'.

Jesus is the laborer and the one that hires other co-laborers for His service in the vineyard. "The kingdom of heaven is like unto a man, an householder, which went out early in the morning to HIRE laborers into His vineyard", Jesus said. And if a laborer could be hired, it goes without saying that the same can be fired. To play on words and alphabets, I could not help but notice that the difference between hired and fired are the letters H and F, which can as well stand for the condition of our heart (H) or our inevitable fall (F) if we choose the path of pride. Hence, the need to keep our heart with all diligence for it as utmost privilege to be among those chosen to serve Him.

"For we are labourers together with God: ye are God's husbandry, ye are God's building." 1 Corinthians 3:9 KJV

"For the kingdom of heaven is like unto a man that is an householder, which went out early in the morning to hire labourers into his vineyard." Matthew 20:1 KJV

"After these things the Lord appointed other seventy also, and sent them two and two before his face into every city and place, whither he himself would come." Luke 10:1 KJV

"We then, as workers together with him, beseech you also that ye receive not the grace of God in vain." 2 Corinthians 6:1 KJV

"Except the Lord build the house, they labour in vain that build it: except the Lord keep the city, the watchman waketh but in vain. It is vain for you to rise up early, to sit up late, to eat the bread of sorrows: for so he giveth his beloved sleep." Psalms 127:1-2 KJV

3. I am only a clay, not the Potter.

Paul made it clear to us that we are like earthen vessels filled with treasure — jars of clay. God told prophet Jeremiah to go to the Potter's house and from there He spoke to him and brought him to some realities about how He sees us. Though He had made us in His own image and likeness, He's the Potter and we are the clay. Can a clay say to the Potter, "this is what l really want"? No. It can never happen! God makes all kinds of vessels as the Potter and designates some to honor and some to dishonor, but if a man purges himself from pride, he shall be a vessel unto honor, sanctified, and meet for the master's use, and prepared unto every good work. It is up to a man to keep himself purified and humble so that he can always fit the criteria of a man God uses.

"The word which came to Jeremiah from the Lord, saying, Arise, and go down to the potter's house, and

there I will cause thee to hear my words. Then I went down to the potter's house, and, behold, he wrought a work on the wheels. And the vessel that he made of clay was marred in the hand of the potter: so he made it again another vessel, as seemed good to the potter to make it. Then the word of the Lord came to me, saying, O house of Israel, cannot I do with you as this potter? saith the Lord. Behold, as the clay is in the potter's hand, so are ye in mine hand, O house of Israel." Jeremiah 18:1-6 KJV

"But in a great house there are not only vessels of gold and of silver, but also of wood and of earth; and some to honour, and some to dishonour. If a man therefore purge himself from these, he shall be a vessel unto honour, sanctified, and meet for the master's use, and prepared unto every good work." 2 Timothy 2:20-21 KJV

4. I am not even on the list of the least Apostles.

Man is like a wild olive branch. With all that we have done in this wonderful heavenly relationship, God still decided out of His kindness and mercy to graft us into the vine as a branch. As a branch, we are not independent but fully dependent on the root, so a man must not and cannot boast of himself as something that he or she is not. The original branch was taken off because of unbelief; they were broken off. Paul attempted to express this mystery when he said "I am crucified with Christ, nevertheless l live, yet not l, but Christ lives in him, and therefore as a result of Christ's intervention, my life in the flesh is by faith in the Son of God." A man that must go far with God must walk in faith and understand that he exists only by the grace of God. Paul said he was the least of the Apostles but by the grace of God, he became what he became. It is absolutely God's grace that enables man to labor with Christ.

> *"And if some of the branches be broken off, and thou, being a wild olive tree, wert grafted in among them, and with them partakest of the root and fatness of the olive tree; Boast not against the branches. But if thou boast, thou bearest not the root, but the root thee. Thou wilt say then, The branches were broken off, that I might be grafted in. Well; because of unbelief they were broken off, and thou standest by faith. Be not high minded, but fear: For if God spared not the natural branches, take heed lest he also spare not thee." Romans 11:17-21 KJV*

> *"I am crucified with Christ: nevertheless I live; yet not I, but Christ liveth in me: and the life which I now live in the flesh I live by the faith of the Son of God, who loved me, and gave himself for me." Galatians 2:20 KJV*

> *"For I am the least of the apostles, that am not meet to be called an apostle, because I persecuted the church of God. But by the grace of God I am what I am: and his grace which was bestowed upon me was not in vain; but I laboured more abundantly than they all: yet not I, but the grace of God which was with me. Therefore whether it were I or they, so we preach, and so ye believed." 1 Corinthians 15:9-11 KJV*

5. I am limited, He's unlimited.

God is unquantifiable, unmeasurable and limitless. These are the attributes of God and what makes God, God. A man on other hand is quantifiable, measurable and limited; outside of God, he cannot exist alone — he only finds purpose in being grafted into the true vine. A man cannot do anything without God because God is the One upholding all things by the Word of His power. A man's word cannot hold any water — cannot even sustain him or her if his or her life depends upon it. Everything a man has was given to him by God — the God that blessed him in the beginning and commanded him to be fruitful, multiply, replenish, subdue and have dominion. How can this limited man become high minded? A man must keep himself or herself grounded by the grace made available by the unlimited God.

> *"I am the true vine, and my Father is the husbandman. Every branch in me that beareth not fruit he taketh away: and every branch that beareth fruit, he purgeth it, that it may bring forth more fruit. Now ye are clean through the word which I have spoken unto you. Abide in me, and I in you. As the branch cannot bear fruit of itself, except it abide in the vine; no more can ye, except ye abide in me. I am the vine, ye are the branches: He that abideth in me, and I in him, the same bringeth forth much fruit: for without me ye can do nothing. If a man abide not in me, he is cast forth as a branch, and is withered; and men gather them, and cast them into the fire, and they are burned. If ye abide in me, and my words abide in you, ye shall ask what ye will, and it shall be done unto you. Herein is my Father glorified, that ye bear much fruit; so shall ye be my disciples." John 15:1-8 KJV*

> *"God, who at sundry times and in divers manners spake in time past unto the fathers by the prophets, Hath in*

these last days spoken unto us by his Son, whom he hath appointed heir of all things, by whom also he made the worlds; Who being the brightness of his glory, and the express image of his person, and upholding all things by the word of his power, when he had by himself purged our sins, sat down on the right hand of the Majesty on high;" Hebrews 1:1-3 KJV

6. I am not a God's sponsor, I give for my own benefit.

A man lives on the principle of seedtime and harvest time; as long as there is a planting season, the harvest season is just around the corner — but he needs to wait for it. God, however, does not need seedtime or harvest time to do whatever He wants to accomplish here on earth or in the heaven. He declared that the silver and gold are His and He owns the cattle upon the thousand hills. God has been before we came and will continue to be after man has long gone. He said I am God, I change not. In other words, God doesn't grow old, cannot be broke, can never be sick, doesn't take a day off...and the list goes on and on. So man is not and can never qualify to become God's sponsor — he is too limited to assume that role! The plan and purpose of God is too big to be financed by man. It is always an opportunity when we are able to give to His work.

"The silver is mine, and the gold is mine, saith the Lord of hosts." Haggai 2:8 KJV

"Hear, O my people, and I will speak; O Israel, and I will testify against thee: I am God, even thy God. I will not reprove thee for thy sacrifices or thy burnt offerings,

to have been continually before me. I will take no bullock out of thy house, nor he goats out of thy folds. For every beast of the forest is mine, and the cattle upon a thousand hills. I know all the fowls of the mountains: and the wild beasts of the field are mine. If I were hungry, I would not tell thee: for the world is mine, and the fulness thereof." Psalms 50:7-12 KJV

"For I am the Lord, I change not; therefore ye sons of Jacob are not consumed." Malachi 3:6 KJV

7. I am not God's father; I am only His child.

I am a child of God, and will remain a child till I see Him face to face. Whenever a man thinks he has grown to the point that he can advise God, then it is time for that man to leave the planet which God created. Solomon told God that he was but a little child: and does not know how to lead His people; he asked God for wisdom and as a result he got more than he bargained for. Look at Jesus Who came from God; He gave us an insight into how unqualified man is to advice God or speak for Him until He's authorized. He said, "Verily, verily, I say unto you, the Son cannot do anything of His own accord" — and this is Jesus talking. He said that He has not spoken for Himself, and that it is God that commands Him on what to say per time. A man in the flesh therefore is not qualified to advise Him. For a man to be used, he must be patient to hear what heaven is saying per time.

"And now, O Lord my God, thou hast made thy servant king instead of David my father: and I am but a little child: I know not how to go out or come in. And thy servant is in the midst of thy people which thou hast

chosen, a great people, that cannot be numbered nor counted for multitude. Give therefore thy servant an understanding heart to judge thy people, that I may discern between good and bad: for who is able to judge this thy so great a people? And the speech pleased the Lord, that Solomon had asked this thing. And God said unto him, Because thou hast asked this thing, and hast not asked for thyself long life; neither hast asked riches for thyself, nor hast asked the life of thine enemies; but hast asked for thyself understanding to discern judgment; Behold, I have done according to thy words: lo, I have given thee a wise and an understanding heart; so that there was none like thee before thee, neither after thee shall any arise like unto thee. And I have also given thee that which thou hast not asked, both riches, and honour: so that there shall not be any among the kings like unto thee all thy days." 1 Kings 3:7-13 KJV

"Then answered Jesus and said unto them, Verily, verily, I say unto you, The Son can do nothing of himself, but what he seeth the Father do: for what things soever he doeth, these also doeth the Son likewise. For the Father loveth the Son, and sheweth him all things that himself doeth: and he will shew him greater works than these, that ye may marvel." John 5:19-20 KJV

"For I have not spoken of myself; but the Father which sent me, he gave me a commandment, what I should say, and what I should speak. And I know that his commandment is life everlasting: whatsoever I speak therefore, even as the Father said unto me, so I speak." John 12:49-50 KJV

8. I am only selected and elected by grace

Esau learnt this hands-on. Nothing qualifies a man for divine election, save the grace of God. It was by grace that we are included in God's plan — we did not choose Him but He chose us to be with Him. God told Rebecca that two nations were in her womb and two manner of people, and He said that one shall be stronger than the other and the elder shall serve the younger. On what basis is this choice? On God basis! He's not accountable to anyone. God chose you and I before the foundation of the world. A man must be thankful for this election by grace by which he is called with a holy calling, out of darkness into God's marvelous light.

> *"And the Lord said unto her, Two nations are in thy womb, and two manner of people shall be separated from thy bowels; and the one people shall be stronger than the other people; and the elder shall serve the younger." Genesis 25:23 KJV*

> *"Ye have not chosen me, but I have chosen you, and ordained you, that ye should go and bring forth fruit, and that your fruit should remain: that whatsoever ye shall ask of the Father in my name, he may give it you." John 15:16 KJV*

> *"According as he hath chosen us in him before the foundation of the world, that we should be holy and without blame before him in love:" Ephesians 1:4 KJV*

> *"But we are bound to give thanks alway to God for you, brethren beloved of the Lord, because God hath from the beginning chosen you to salvation through sanctification of the Spirit and belief of the truth:" 2 Thessalonians 2:13 KJV*

"Who hath saved us, and called us with an holy calling, not according to our works, but according to his own purpose and grace, which was given us in Christ Jesus before the world began," 2 Timothy 1:9 KJV

CHAPTER TEN

GOD'S ORIGINAL CREATION

God is an architect, a designer and a creator. He made every man unique as a masterpiece — no two creations are the same. He told Jeremiah that before He formed him in the belly, He knew him intimately. David praised God because he reckoned that he was fearfully and wonderfully created. He went into a little details of how God made him unique. David said that his substance was not hidden from God. Man is such a special creation that the creation of each of us was a covert operation. God curiously made us without the knowledge of the angels — and that made them jealous of man, and God made them ministering spirits to minister to man.

Jesus raised the stakes in our redemption and by so doing, made us better masterpieces by His blood and created us anew. Hence what Paul said in 2 Corinthians 5:17, that if any man is in Christ, he is a masterpiece, old things are passed away, and behold, all things are now new. A man can now do good things which God had planned for him to do before the foundation of the world.

> *"Before I formed thee in the belly I knew thee; and before thou camest forth out of the womb I sanctified thee, and I ordained thee a prophet unto the nations." Jeremiah 1:5 KJV*

> *"For thou hast possessed my reins: thou hast covered me in my mother's womb. I will praise thee; for I am fearfully and wonderfully made: marvellous are thy works; and that my soul knoweth right well. My substance was not hid from thee, when I was made in secret, and curiously wrought in the lowest parts of the earth. Thine eyes did see my substance, yet being unperfect; and in thy book all my members were written, which in continuance were fashioned, when as yet there was none of them." Psalms 139:13-16 KJV*

> *"Oh yes, you shaped me first inside, then out; you formed me in my mother's womb. I thank you, High God—you're breathtaking! Body and soul, I am marvelously made! I worship in adoration—what a creation! You know me inside and out, you know every bone in my body; You know exactly how I was made, bit by bit, how I was sculpted from nothing into something. Like an open book, you watched me grow from conception to birth; all the stages of my life were spread out before you, The days of my life all prepared before I'd even lived one day." Psalm 139:13-16 MSG*

> *"For we are God's masterpiece. He has created us anew in Christ Jesus, so we can do the good things he planned for us long ago." Ephesians 2:10 NLT*

I was looking for what makes a man unique when l found an article written by Kelsey Kloss about the nine body parts that are unique to each of us like our fingerprints, copied and published with permission. It is so interesting that l could not remove or add anything to it. Enjoy as you read and rediscover how precious it is to be one-in-seven-billion unique.

NINE BODY PARTS AS UNIQUE AS YOUR FINGERPRINT[1]

You're one in a million (or, uh, 7 billion), and these special characteristics prove it.

1. Iris

Eyes are the window to your soul and your identity. The iris, a muscle that opens and closes the pupil to control how much light enters the eye, has tiny textural patterns. DNA determines the color and structure of the iris, but its random pits, furrows, swirls, and rifts occur during fetal development, which makes every iris unique (even your two irises don't match each other). The patterns are thought to appear as the fetus opens and closes its developing eyes, and iris tissues tighten and fold.

2. Ear

Trace the rim of your ear: Feel those curves and ridges? You're the only person in the world with that exact shape. In one British study, researchers developed an algorithm

1 See https://www.rd.com/health/wellness/unique-body-parts/

that could identify a single individual out of more than 250 others with a 99.6 percent accuracy rate by analyzing how light reflects off the curves of the ears. The ear is such a handy identifier that Yahoo is developing technology to unlock smartphones with an ear scanner. Someone receiving a call would unlock the phone by simply pressing it to the ear.

3. Lip Print

Hypothetically, detectives could seal evidence with a kiss. A study in the Journal of Forensic Dental Sciences found that the pattern of elevations and depressions in the lips are as unique as fingerprints. There's just one problem: Though lip prints have been used as identification in the court in isolated cases, criminals typically don't smooch crime scenes.

4. Tongue

Like a fingerprint, the tongue has its own shape and texture, and its tiny bumps and ridges are distributed in a way that is uniquely yours. These patterns rarely change over time since the tongue is protected inside the mouth (unlike fingertips, which may become scarred). Researchers are developing 3D tongue imaging to aid in identification.

(See https://www.rd.com/health/wellness/unique-body-parts/)

5. Voice

Ok, so it's not quite a body part, but your voice is unlike anyone else's. Some vocal characteristics are easy to detect, such as frequency (high or low) and intensity (loud or soft). Other traits, however, such as tightness, resonance, or nasality are usually more difficult to pinpoint. An individual's unique vocal tract is partly genetic and partly learned. The length of one's neck and the width of the pharynx plays a part, but so do learned characteristics such as lip rounding and vowel pronunciation. Based on these combined traits, scientists have already created systems to automatically recognize a person's voice if it is pre-recorded in a database.

6. Toe Print

A fetus's toe prints develop at the same time as fingerprints, and are just as unique. Since crooks are more likely to leave fingerprints behind, the FBI maintains a national database that links 66 million people to their fingerprints, but does not record foot or toe prints. In one classic case, however, a toe print was used in court when a burglar broke into a Scottish bakery and left a print on the flour-dusted floor. Though it was the only evidence against the criminal, the jury convicted him within 15 minutes.

7. Teeth

Your teeth not only reveal your DNA—which is why dental records are often used to identify bodies—but are particular to you based on your personal habits. Perhaps you clench your jaw, grind your teeth, play a certain instrument, or hold keys in your mouth on the way to the car. Because of this environmental wear and tear, even identical twins have different sets of teeth.

8. Retina

The very back of the eye, the retina, is a precise snapshot of your nervous system, unique to you. It displays a pattern of blood vessels that your eye doctor observes to detect the first signs of diabetes, high blood pressure, and even declining brain health. Though human retinas are typically only observed at the optometrist, retina identification is widely used in the animal world to verify show cattle and purebred horses and to track disease outbreaks.

9. Gait

OK, it's not quite your feet—but how you use them. Do you slightly drag one foot? Bounce on another? Even if you've never noticed anything unusual about how you stroll, sophisticated systems can. When an international team of bioengineers analyzed the foot pressure patterns of more than 100 participants, they identified individuals with a 99.6 percent accuracy rate. Though more research is needed, gait identification could eventually be a way of identifying individuals from a distance—such as camera footage that identifies a robber walking out of a bank.

We were made to be unique and not to copy or compare ourselves with someone else. Paul had the revelation of the danger of comparing ourselves to others. Comparing does only one damage: it dilutes the original content of your God given characteristics! Instead of comparing, we should renew our mind to be transformed and to prove what is good, and acceptable, and the perfect will of God — that is reaching the full measure of the stature of Christ.

> *"For we dare not make ourselves of the number, or compare ourselves with some that commend themselves: but they measuring themselves by themselves, and comparing themselves among themselves, are not wise." 2 Corinthians 10:12 KJV*

> *"And be not conformed to this world: but be ye transformed by the renewing of your mind, that ye may prove what is that good, and acceptable, and perfect, will of God." Romans 12:2 KJV*

CHAPTER ELEVEN

THE MAN WITH ANSWERS

This book was conceived after so much meditation on the question that King Solomon asked when he was dedicating the temple. He said; "But will God in very deed dwell with men on earth?" Then king Solomon went on to try to describe the awesomeness of God — how big and large this God is. From the new testament, we know that God is not only willing to dwell with man, but longs to dwell in man. King Solomon prayed to God for the temple he built in Jerusalem that God should keep His eyes upon all the requests made thereof. Likewise, Christ has prayed for and continues to pray for us as our high priest. As a result, it is only logical to juxtapose the effects of Solomon's prayer on the temple and the result of Jesus' prayer for His temple (which is man).

> *"But will God in very deed dwell with men on the earth? behold, heaven and the heaven of heavens cannot contain thee; how much less this house which I have built!" 2 Chronicles 6:18 KJV*

"To whom coming, as unto a living stone, disallowed indeed of men, but chosen of God, and precious, Ye also, as lively stones, are built up a spiritual house, an holy priesthood, to offer up spiritual sacrifices, acceptable to God by Jesus Christ." 1 Peter 2:4-5 KJV

"Have respect therefore to the prayer of thy servant, and to his supplication, O Lord my God, to hearken unto the cry and the prayer which thy servant prayeth before thee: That thine eyes may be open upon this house day and night, upon the place whereof thou hast said that thou wouldest put thy name there; to hearken unto the prayer which thy servant prayeth toward this place." 2 Chronicles 6:19-20 KJV

"Neither pray I for these alone, but for them also which shall believe on me through their word; That they all may be one; as thou, Father, art in me, and I in thee, that they also may be one in us: that the world may believe that thou hast sent me. And the glory which thou gavest me I have given them; that they may be one, even as we are one: I in them, and thou in me, that they may be made perfect in one; and that the world may know that thou hast sent me, and hast loved them, as thou hast loved me." John 17:20-23 KJV

Let us do a brief exegesis of 2 Chronicles 6:21-42 — twenty two verses that shows the capacity of a man in whom God dwells.

VERSE 21

"Hearken therefore unto the supplications of thy servant, and of thy people Israel, which they shall make toward this place: hear thou from thy dwelling place, even from

heaven; and when thou hearest, forgive." 2 Chronicles 6:21 KJV

King Solomon asked God to answer any prayer that shall be made toward the temple. As such, anytime anyone prays toward the temple, there is a guarantee for that prayer to be answered. Now, we are that temple in whom God dwells, therefore every prayer we pray according to His will is guaranteed an answer. What Isaiah prophesied in Isaiah 65 has now come to pass; Jesus has already come, so this promise of answered prayers is now active, that before we call unto God, He will answer and while we are yet speaking, he will hear.

"And it shall come to pass, that before they call, I will answer; and while they are yet speaking, I will hear." Isaiah 65:24 KJV

VERSES 22 AND 23

"If a man sin against his neighbour, and an oath be laid upon him to make him swear, and the oath come before thine altar in this house; Then hear thou from heaven, and do, and judge thy servants, by requiting the wicked, by recompensing his way upon his own head; and by justifying the righteous, by giving him according to his righteousness." 2 Chronicles 6:22-23 KJV

King Solomon called for God to defend His name when an issue is brought to the altar — to execute justice on the wicked and recompense the righteous. In this dispensation, for a man in whom God dwells, God on his inside has assured, "Vengeance is mine, and I will repay."

> *"Recompense to no man evil for evil. Provide things honest in the sight of all men. If it be possible, as much as lieth in you, live peaceably with all men. Dearly beloved, avenge not yourselves, but rather give place unto wrath: for it is written, Vengeance is mine; I will repay, saith the Lord." Romans 12:17-19 KJV*

VERSES 24 AND 25

> *"And if thy people Israel be put to the worse before the enemy, because they have sinned against thee; and shall return and confess thy name, and pray and make supplication before thee in this house; Then hear thou from the heavens, and forgive the sin of thy people Israel, and bring them again unto the land which thou gavest to them and to their fathers." 2 Chronicles 6:24-25 KJV*

King Solomon asked God to forgive the sins of the people when they come to this house and confess the name of the Lord. He also asked that as a result of their forgiveness, there should be a restoration. A man in whom God dwells is a new creation. When he or she sins, there's grace and mercy available for full restoration.

> *"For we have not an high priest which cannot be touched with the feeling of our infirmities; but was in all points tempted like as we are, yet without sin. Let us therefore come boldly unto the throne of grace, that we may obtain mercy, and find grace to help in time of need." Hebrews 4:15-16 KJV*

VERSES 26 AND 27

"When the heaven is shut up, and there is no rain, because they have sinned against thee; yet if they pray toward this place, and confess thy name, and turn from their sin, when thou dost afflict them; Then hear thou from heaven, and forgive the sin of thy servants, and of thy people Israel, when thou hast taught them the good way, wherein they should walk; and send rain upon thy land, which thou hast given unto thy people for an inheritance." 2 Chronicles 6:26-27 KJV

King Solomon asked God to send prosperity instead of scarcity that might be as a result of sin. The God that dwells in man does not tempt any man with evil; He does not punish us with evil; even when we do err, He always provides a way of escape out of trouble for a man in whom He dwells.

"There hath no temptation taken you but such as is common to man: but God is faithful, who will not suffer you to be tempted above that ye are able; but will with the temptation also make a way to escape, that ye may be able to bear it." 1 Corinthians 10:13 KJV

VERSES 28 TO 31

"If there be dearth in the land, if there be pestilence, if there be blasting, or mildew, locusts, or caterpillars; if their enemies besiege them in the cities of their land; whatsoever sore or whatsoever sickness there be: Then what prayer or what supplication soever shall be made of any man, or of all thy people Israel, when every one shall know his own sore and his own grief, and shall

spread forth his hands in this house: Then hear thou from heaven thy dwelling place, and forgive, and render unto every man according unto all his ways, whose heart thou knowest; (for thou only knowest the hearts of the children of men:) That they may fear thee, to walk in thy ways, so long as they live in the land which thou gavest unto our fathers." 2 Chronicles 6:28-31 KJV

King Solomon asked God for deliverance from the oppression of the enemy. If any man shall pray toward the temple, that God should hear from heaven and deliver. A man in whom God dwells automatically receives divine protection. Even when he or she becomes a lawful captive, God promises deliverance first and correction later.

"Shall the prey be taken from the mighty, or the lawful captive delivered? But thus saith the Lord, Even the captives of the mighty shall be taken away, and the prey of the terrible shall be delivered: for I will contend with him that contendeth with thee, and I will save thy children." Isaiah 49:24-25 KJV

VERSES 32 AND 33

"Moreover concerning the stranger, which is not of thy people Israel, but is come from a far country for thy great name's sake, and thy mighty hand, and thy stretched out arm; if they come and pray in this house; Then hear thou from the heavens, even from thy dwelling place, and do according to all that the stranger calleth to thee for; that all people of the earth may know thy name, and fear thee, as doth thy people Israel, and may know that this house which I have built is called by thy name." 2 Chronicles 6:32-33 KJV

King Solomon asked God to answer the prayer of strangers that are not of the commonwealth of Israel, and God has done that many times before in the Bible. A man in whom God dwells is no longer a stranger alienated from God, but has been accepted into the beloved by adoption through Jesus Christ.

> *"Now therefore ye are no more strangers and foreigners, but fellow citizens with the saints, and of the household of God;" Ephesians 2:19 KJV*

VERSES 34 AND 35

> *"If thy people go out to war against their enemies by the way that thou shalt send them, and they pray unto thee toward this city which thou hast chosen, and the house which I have built for thy name; Then hear thou from the heavens their prayer and their supplication, and maintain their cause." 2 Chronicles 6:34-35 KJV*

King Solomon asked God to fight for His people when at war, to answer for them when they pray toward the temple and to destroy their adversaries. God has done that many times in the Bible. A man in whom God dwells does not war according to the flesh, however. The God on the inside fights with weapons that are not carnal, but mighty through God for pulling down strongholds and casting down imaginations.

> *"For though we walk in the flesh, we do not war after the flesh: (For the weapons of our warfare are not carnal, but mighty through God to the pulling down of strong holds;) Casting down imaginations, and every high thing*

that exalteth itself against the knowledge of God, and bringing into captivity every thought to the obedience of Christ;" 2 Corinthians 10:3-5 KJV

VERSES 36 TO 39

"If they sin against thee, (for there is no man which sinneth not,) and thou be angry with them, and deliver them over before their enemies, and they carry them away captives unto a land far off or near; Yet if they bethink themselves in the land whither they are carried captive, and turn and pray unto thee in the land of their captivity, saying, We have sinned, we have done amiss, and have dealt wickedly; If they return to thee with all their heart and with all their soul in the land of their captivity, whither they have carried them captives, and pray toward their land, which thou gavest unto their fathers, and toward the city which thou hast chosen, and toward the house which I have built for thy name: Then hear thou from the heavens, even from thy dwelling place, their prayer and their supplications, and maintain their cause, and forgive thy people which have sinned against thee." 2 Chronicles 6:36-39 KJV

King Solomon asked God to save the children from their enemies, even from sin that kindles the anger of God against them, and God has done that times without number. A man in whom God dwells understands however that even when he or she sins, the gifts and calling of God are without repentance. What a big difference between the God that dwells with men and the One that dwells in men.

"For the gifts and calling of God are without repentance." Romans 11:29 KJV

VERSES 40 TO 42

"Now, my God, let, I beseech thee, thine eyes be open, and let thine ears be attent unto the prayer that is made in this place. Now therefore arise, O Lord God, into thy resting place, thou, and the ark of thy strength: let thy priests, O Lord God, be clothed with salvation, and let thy saints rejoice in goodness. O Lord God, turn not away the face of thine anointed: remember the mercies of David thy servant." 2 Chronicles 6:40-42 KJV

King Solomon finalized his prayer by asking God to come and dwell in the temple, for God to arise and come into His resting place, into the ark of His strength. All these prayers will be in vain if God did not dwell in that temple — all the prayers, restoration and deliverances will be impossible. A man that wants to see God come into His dwelling place must ask Jesus to come into his or her heart. (We call this the prayer of salvation). Such a man will be translated from the company of the people whom God dwells with to the company of the people in whom God dwells.

"But what saith it? The word is nigh thee, even in thy mouth, and in thy heart: that is, the word of faith, which we preach; That if thou shalt confess with thy mouth the Lord Jesus, and shalt believe in thine heart that God hath raised him from the dead, thou shalt be saved. For with the heart man believeth unto righteousness; and with the mouth confession is made unto salvation. For the scripture saith, Whosoever believeth on him shall not be ashamed." Romans 10:8-11 KJV

CHAPTER TWELVE
A PRAISING MACHINE

A man in whom God dwells is like a radio that is always humming and producing melodies to his or her God. From all we have seen and studied about the man in whom God dwells, we can easily summarize such a man as follows; a carrier of God, a representative of God, an enforcer of God's will, a mouthpiece of God, a commander of God's army, the epitome of God's power, the custodian of all of God's resources, the closer of God's plan, the epitome of God's creation, an original creation and an answer to all earthly needs.

So why must such a person be given to the praise and worship of God?

Psalms 150:6 says "Let everything that has breath praise the Lord…" This man has the divine breath in his nostrils and should therefore praise God regardless of his/her situation and circumstances. Moreover, God dwells in His kingdom and the scripture reveals to us that the kingdom of God is neither here nor there but rather within us.

The one thing that constantly goes on in heaven is praise and worship. Revelation 4:8 tells us that the four beasts had each of them six wings about him, and they were full of eyes within, and they rest not day and night, saying, "Holy, holy, holy, Lord God Almighty, which was, and is, and is to come." They continually gave glory to Him that sits on the throne and the twenty four elders keep falling down before Him and casting their crowns before the throne saying, "He's worthy to receive glory,and honor and power."

Apart from the four beasts and the twenty four elders, there are innumerable angels in heaven and their only assignment is to praise God constantly and continuously. Such was the main responsibility of lucifer before he was cast out of heaven — to lead the angelic hosts to offer worship to Him that sits on the throne forever. Apostle John heard the voices of many angels round about the throne, the number of them were ten thousand, and thousands of thousands — and to think that all of this is going on in a man whose heart has become God's throne! How can that man not praise and worship God at all times?

In Psalms 34:1, David said "I will praise the Lord at all times; His praise shall continually be in my mouth". Could this have contributed to why God calls him 'a man after my heart'? God is still looking for men after His heart in this dispensation, my question to you is WILL YOU BE ONE OF THEM?

> *"And the four beasts had each of them six wings about him; and they were full of eyes within: and they rest not day and night, saying, Holy, holy, holy, Lord God*

Almighty, which was, and is, and is to come. And when those beasts give glory and honour and thanks to him that sat on the throne, who liveth for ever and ever, The four and twenty elders fall down before him that sat on the throne, and worship him that liveth for ever and ever, and cast their crowns before the throne, saying, Thou art worthy, O Lord, to receive glory and honour and power: for thou hast created all things, and for thy pleasure they are and were created." Revelation 4:8-11 KJV

"And I beheld, and I heard the voice of many angels round about the throne and the beasts and the elders: and the number of them was ten thousand times ten thousand, and thousands of thousands; Saying with a loud voice, Worthy is the Lamb that was slain to receive power, and riches, and wisdom, and strength, and honour, and glory, and blessing. And every creature which is in heaven, and on the earth, and under the earth, and such as are in the sea, and all that are in them, heard I saying, Blessing, and honour, and glory, and power, be unto him that sitteth upon the throne, and unto the Lamb for ever and ever. And the four beasts said, Amen. And the four and twenty elders fell down and worshipped him that liveth for ever and ever." Revelation 5:11-14 KJV

"I will bless the Lord at all times: his praise shall continually be in my mouth." Psalms 34:1 KJV

JEHOSHAPHAT AND HIS PRAISE ARMY

King Jehoshaphat was confronted with such an opposition that he cannot overcome by physical and natural strength.

Three kings had come together to fight and displace Judah from their inheritance. In the midst of the opposition, he did what most seasoned warriors will never do: he assembled a praise and worship team to go in front of the battle and the unusual happened. Victory erupted as a result of singing and praising God.

He wasn't the first. His forefathers had wrought victory in battle by praising God. Praising God brings God's hand down for He inhabits the praises of His people. A man in whom God dwells have answers to any battle of life by just turning on what is domicile in him or her, even the power of praise and worship.

> *"Then there came some that told Jehoshaphat, saying, There cometh a great multitude against thee from beyond the sea on this side Syria; and, behold, they be in Hazazon–tamar, which is En–gedi. And Jehoshaphat bowed his head with his face to the ground: and all Judah and the inhabitants of Jerusalem fell before the Lord, worshipping the Lord. And the Levites, of the children of the Kohathites, and of the children of the Korhites, stood up to praise the Lord God of Israel with a loud voice on high. And they rose early in the morning, and went forth into the wilderness of Tekoa: and as they went forth, Jehoshaphat stood and said, Hear me, O Judah, and ye inhabitants of Jerusalem; Believe in the Lord your God, so shall ye be established; believe his prophets, so shall ye prosper. And when he had consulted with the people, he appointed singers unto the Lord, and that should praise the beauty of holiness, as they went out before the army, and to say, Praise the Lord; for his mercy endureth for ever. And when they began to sing and to praise, the Lord set ambushments against the*

children of Ammon, Moab, and mount Seir, which were come against Judah; and they were smitten. For the children of Ammon and Moab stood up against the inhabitants of mount Seir, utterly to slay and destroy them: and when they had made an end of the inhabitants of Seir, every one helped to destroy another." 2 Chronicles 20:2, 18-23 KJV

DAVID DANCING AWAY

David's insatiable appetite for praising and worshipping God made him a man after God's heart. While we may not know how and when David learnt about praising God, we do know that he spent a good portion of his youth as a Shepherd tending his father's sheep. He learnt to praise God for protection while he confronted the bear and the lion; he praised God for provision for the sheep; praised God for provision for his family and many more. On one occasion, he danced so violently before his God that one of his wife mocked him.

"And David danced before the Lord with all his might; and David was girded with a linen ephod. So David and all the house of Israel brought up the ark of the Lord with shouting, and with the sound of the trumpet. And as the ark of the Lord came into the city of David, Michal Saul's daughter looked through a window, and saw king David leaping and dancing before the Lord; and she despised him in her heart. And they brought in the ark of the Lord, and set it in his place, in the midst of the tabernacle that David had pitched for it: and David offered burnt offerings and peace offerings before the Lord." 2 Samuel 6:14-17 KJV

> *"Then David returned to bless his household. And Michal the daughter of Saul came out to meet David, and said, How glorious was the king of Israel to day, who uncovered himself to day in the eyes of the handmaids of his servants, as one of the vain fellows shamelessly uncovereth himself! And David said unto Michal, It was before the Lord, which chose me before thy father, and before all his house, to appoint me ruler over the people of the Lord, over Israel: therefore will I play before the Lord. And I will yet be more vile than thus, and will be base in mine own sight: and of the maidservants which thou hast spoken of, of them shall I be had in honour." 2 Samuel 6:20-22 KJV*

A man in whom God dwells must be a dancer for his God.

SOLOMON IN WORSHIP

King Solomon was a true son of his father. Solomon was borne out of a relationship that almost destroyed the house of David — which tells us by the way that it does not matter where you have been, or what you have done, when God is domicile in you, your worship can bring the glory of God down. King Solomon was dedicating the house he built for the Lord and the ark was brought to its resting place, then he commanded the Levites with their instruments. When the trumpeters and singers were making one sound (in worship) in praising and thanking the Lord, and when they lifted up their voices, saying "for the Lord is good and His mercies endures forever," suddenly the house was filled with a CLOUD OF GLORY — the glory of God was so heavy upon the temple that the priests could not stand to minister by the reason of the cloud: for the GLORY OF THE LORD had filled the house. A man in whom God dwells can manifest God's glory on demand through the instrumentality of praise.

"There was nothing in the ark save the two tables which Moses put therein at Horeb, when the Lord made a covenant with the children of Israel, when they came out of Egypt. And it came to pass, when the priests were come out of the holy place: (for all the priests that were present were sanctified, and did not then wait by course: Also the Levites which were the singers, all of them of Asaph, of Heman, of Jeduthun, with their sons and their brethren, being arrayed in white linen, having cymbals and psalteries and harps, stood at the east end of the altar, and with them an hundred and twenty priests sounding with trumpets:) It came even to pass, as the trumpeters and singers were as one, to make one sound to be heard in praising and thanking the Lord; and when they lifted up their voice with the trumpets and cymbals and instruments of musick, and praised the Lord, saying, For he is good; for his mercy endureth for ever: that then the house was filled with a cloud, even the house of the Lord; So that the priests could not stand to minister by reason of the cloud: for the glory of the Lord had filled the house of God." 2 Chronicles 5:10-14 KJV

ABRAHAM IN SACRIFICE

Obedience is an act of worship and as far as obedience goes, Abraham is indeed an exemplary Bible character. He became God's friend and entered into an everlasting covenant with God because he understood what true worship really meant through sacrifice. Abraham took the wood for the burnt offering, and laid it upon Isaac his son — their only son, the heir of promise. Abraham bound Isaac up and laid him upon the wood to give God his all in worship through sacrificial giving and God called him and honored Abraham. A man in whom God dwells will always hear God's call through his or her sacrificial worship of the most High. As you honor God in worship through your giving, may heaven respond rapidly to you.

> *"And Abraham took the wood of the burnt offering, and laid it upon Isaac his son; and he took the fire in his hand, and a knife; and they went both of them together. And Isaac spake unto Abraham his father, and said, My father: and he said, Here am I, my son. And he said, Behold the fire and the wood: but where is the lamb for a burnt offering? And Abraham said, My son, God will provide himself a lamb for a burnt offering: so they went both of them together. And they came to the place which God had told him of; and Abraham built an altar there, and laid the wood in order, and bound Isaac his son, and laid him on the altar upon the wood. And Abraham stretched forth his hand, and took the knife to slay his son. And the angel of the Lord called unto him out of heaven, and said, Abraham, Abraham: and he said, Here am I." Genesis 22:6-11 KJV*

HOW TO PRAISE GOD

1. Praise Him With Singing

David, knowing the power of praise and how we can use it as a means of access to God's presence, encourages all the saints to sing unto the Lord, and give thanks at the remembrance of His acts and divine performances. A perfect of example of this is well demonstrated when the children of Israel crossed over the Red Sea. Miriam, the sister of Moses, bursted into singing and the people joined in. The wordings of their song revealed the act of God's holiness: "Who is like unto thee, O Lord, among the gods? Who is like thee, glorious in holiness, fearful in praises, doing wonders." A man in whom God dwells must sing unto the Lord if he wants to see the acts of God's holiness on demand.

> *"Sing unto the Lord, O ye saints of his, and give thanks at the remembrance of his holiness." Psalms 30:4 KJV*

> *"The enemy said, I will pursue, I will overtake, I will divide the spoil; my lust shall be satisfied upon them; I will draw my sword, my hand shall destroy them. Thou didst blow with thy wind, the sea covered them: they sank as lead in the mighty waters. Who is like unto thee, O Lord, among the gods? who is like thee, glorious in holiness, fearful in praises, doing wonders? And Miriam the prophetess, the sister of Aaron, took a timbrel in her hand; and all the women went out after her with timbrels and with dances. And Miriam answered them, Sing ye to the Lord, for he hath triumphed gloriously; the horse and his rider hath he thrown into the sea." Exodus 15:9-11, 20-21 KJV*

2. Praise Him With Worship

David understood the power of worship so much. In one of his songs, he says that he praises God seven times daily. In another, he said that he will praise God continually. We know him to be the only one in the scriptures that got to choose what kind of chastisement he was to receive. He wrote many Psalms in the Bible and one of my favorites is Psalm 99 that says "The Lord reigns; let the people and the earth tremble in worship of the King of kings and the Lord of lords."

A perfect example of how worshipping God can cause the foundation of the whole earth to shake is found the book of Acts chapter 16, when Paul and Silas were detained in the prison. According to Luke, Paul and Silas prayed at midnight and sang praises unto God as an act of worship, and suddenly there was a great earthquake, so that the foundations of the prison were shaken and the doors were opened and everyone's band were loosed. When a man in who God dwells worships God, it causes the voice of God to be heard all over the universe, and we know from scriptures that the voice of the Lord is powerful, and full of majesty — so powerful that it breaks the cedars of Lebanon.

> *"The Lord reigneth; let the people tremble: he sitteth between the cherubims; let the earth be moved. The Lord is great in Zion; and he is high above all the people. Let them praise thy great and terrible name; for it is holy. Exalt the Lord our God, and worship at his holy hill; for the Lord our God is holy." Psalms 99:1-3, 9 KJV*

> *"Give unto the Lord, O ye mighty, give unto the Lord glory and strength. Give unto the Lord the glory due unto his name; worship the Lord in the beauty of holiness. The voice of the Lord is upon the waters: the God of glory thundereth: the Lord is upon many waters. The voice of the Lord is powerful; the voice of the Lord is full of majesty." Psalms 29:1-4 KJV*

> *"And at midnight Paul and Silas prayed, and sang praises unto God: and the prisoners heard them. And suddenly there was a great earthquake, so that the foundations of the prison were shaken: and immediately all the doors were opened, and every one's bands were loosed. And the keeper of the prison awaking out of his sleep, and seeing the prison doors open, he drew out his sword, and would have killed himself, supposing that the prisoners had been fled." Acts 16:25-27 KJV*

3. Praise Him With Dancing

Still gleaning from David's life, we read of how he danced shamelessly before his God. He danced so passionately that Michal the daughter of Saul mocked and despised him. He wrote in Psalms 149:1, "Let them praise His name in the dance…" Note that he did not say a dance but the dance — the dance that brought him deliverance over Goliath. After David defeated Goliath, the women of all the cities came out singing and dancing — quite possibly in response to David's dance of worship. There are numerous examples in the Bible of people who engaged God in the dance and saw a dramatic move of God. A man in whom God dwells must engage in the dance that moves God to action on his behalf.

> *"Let them praise his name in the dance: let them sing praises unto him with the timbrel and harp. For the Lord taketh pleasure in his people: he will beautify the meek with salvation. Let the saints be joyful in glory: let them sing aloud upon their beds. Let the high praises of God be in their mouth, and a two edged sword in their hand; To execute vengeance upon the heathen, and*

punishments upon the people; To bind their kings with chains, and their nobles with fetters of iron; To execute upon them the judgment written: this honour have all his saints. Praise ye the Lord." Psalms 149:3-9 KJV

"And it came to pass as they came, when David was returned from the slaughter of the Philistine, that the women came out of all cities of Israel, singing and dancing, to meet king Saul, with tabrets, with joy, and with instruments of musick." 1 Samuel 18:6 KJV

4. Praise Him With Instruments

Not only was David a good composer, he was also skillful on musical instruments. I like to think of David as the 'Apostle Paul' of the old testament — a man of depth and revelation especially in the worship of our God. He wrote in Psalms 150 "...praise him with the sound of trumpet, psaltery, harp, timbrel, organs and stringed instruments." As a man that knows how to make melody with all kind of instruments, he was able to bring the presence of God down many times with instruments when king Saul comes under the torment of evil spirit. When David plays the harp, Saul was immediately refreshed and well, and the evil spirit departs from him. A man in whom God dwells can cast out evil spirit by just engaging God with musical instruments — you can start with something as simple as a tambourine or just clapping your hands.

"Praise ye the Lord. Praise God in his sanctuary: praise him in the firmament of his power. Praise him for his mighty acts: praise him according to his excellent greatness. Praise him with the sound of the trumpet:

praise him with the psaltery and harp. Praise him with the timbrel and dance: praise him with stringed instruments and organs. Praise him upon the loud cymbals: praise him upon the high sounding cymbals. Let everything that hath breath praise the Lord. Praise ye the Lord." Psalms 150:1-6 KJV

"And Saul sent to Jesse, saying, Let David, I pray thee, stand before me; for he hath found favour in my sight. And it came to pass, when the evil spirit from God was upon Saul, that David took an harp, and played with his hand: so Saul was refreshed, and was well, and the evil spirit departed from him." 1 Samuel 16:22-23 KJV

5. Praise Him With Offering

We turn to David one final time to glean praise and worship lessons from him because he was well-rounded in this regards. He knows how to touch and move the heart of God with his offering and sacrificial giving. He knew that it was a privilege to be able to give to God who owns the cattle upon a thousand hills. When he was preparing for the building of the temple, he said "We thank thee, and praise thy glorious name, but who am l, and what is my people that we should be able to offer so willingly after this sort?" He was also the man reputed for refusing to offer to God that which will not cost him anything. Araunah offered him the land as a gift but he refused and told him that he must buy it from Araunah at a price, because he would not offer burnt offerings unto God from that which does not cost him anything. A man in whom God dwells must be willing to give sacrificially so as to provoke heavenly blessings within him.

"Both riches and honour come of thee, and thou reignest over all; and in thine hand is power and might; and in thine hand it is to make great, and to give strength unto all. Now therefore, our God, we thank thee, and praise thy glorious name. But who am I, and what is my people, that we should be able to offer so willingly after this sort? for all things come of thee, and of thine own have we given thee. For we are strangers before thee, and sojourners, as were all our fathers: our days on the earth are as a shadow, and there is none abiding. O Lord our God, all this store that we have prepared to build thee an house for thine holy name cometh of thine hand, and is all thine own." 1 Chronicles 29:12-16 KJV

"And Araunah said, Wherefore is my lord the king come to his servant? And David said, To buy the threshingfloor of thee, to build an altar unto the Lord, that the plague may be stayed from the people. And Araunah said unto David, Let my lord the king take and offer up what seemeth good unto him: behold, here be oxen for burnt sacrifice, and threshing instruments and other instruments of the oxen for wood. All these things did Araunah, as a king, give unto the king. And Araunah said unto the king, The Lord thy God accept thee. And the king said unto Araunah, Nay; but I will surely buy it of thee at a price: neither will I offer burnt offerings unto the Lord my God of that which doth cost me nothing. So David bought the threshingfloor and the oxen for fifty shekels of silver. And David built there an altar unto the Lord, and offered burnt offerings and peace offerings. So the Lord was entreated for the land, and the plague was stayed from Israel." 2 Samuel 24:21-25 KJV

> Finally, *"a man in whom God dwells must be standing while others are sitting, and outstanding while others are standing, and must be a standard while others are outstanding. That's an heritage of a man in whom God dwells." —Unknown Author*

May that person be you.

ABOUT THE AUTHOR

Dr. Olalekan Joseph Olowe is a physical therapist by trade and a pastor by calling. Together with his wife, Omolade, they are the Presiding Servants over Kingdom Dominion Ministry International (KDMI) with a ministry base at El Paso, Texas from where they reach out globally.

A graduate of Rocky Mountain University of Health Professionals with a transitional Doctorate in Physical Therapy, Joseph is blessed with a physical therapy practice in El Paso, Texas.

He's a prolific writer and the author of I Am Three Dimensional, Living Free: The Power of Self-Control amongst other books. He's happily married to Omolade and they are blessed with three children.

KINGDOM DOMINION MINISTRY INTERNATIONAL (KDMI)

To partner with us or to be part of Kingdom Dominion Ministry International (KDMI), please call or write us

1800-561-9170 or +1 915-478-8807

P. O Box 10499
El Paso, TX 79995

info@hisdominion.org | www.hisdominion.org